D1567134

WINDOWS A

THE ART OF

GENE MOORE

By Judith Goldman with Commentary by Gene Moore

HARRY N. ABRAMS, INC., PUBLISHERS, NEW YORK

Project Director: Lena Tabori
Editor: Ruth Eisenstein
Designer: Dirk Luykx

Note: Unless otherwise indicated, the windows illustrated are Tiffany & Co.
display windows. The list beginning on page 217 gives the date of installation,
with the name of the contributing artist, if any.

Library of Congress Cataloging in Publication Data
Moore, Gene.
    Windows at Tiffany's.
    1. Show-windows.   2. Jewelry trade.   I. Goldman,
Judith.   II. Title.
HF5849.J4M66   659.1'57   80-14261
ISBN 0-8109-1655-X

Library of Congress Catalog Card Number: 80-14261
Illustrations © 1980 Gene Moore. Text © 1980 Harry N. Abrams, B.V.

Printed and bound in Japan

CONTENTS

When I asked Gene Moore to be the Window Display Director of Tiffany & Co., he said to me, "What do you want me to do?"

My reply was, "Gene, I want you to make our windows as beautiful as you can according to your own taste, in which I have complete confidence. Also, don't tell me ahead of time what you are going to do, because that will merely frustrate you. Above all, don't try to sell anything; we'll take care of that in the store."

It was the work of Gene Moore that brought about the realization that the art of window display has been seriously handicapped by the desire of many store managements to have their windows used primarily to sell merchandise and nothing more. It was Gene Moore who released window display artists from the narrowness of this view by demonstrating that windows can enhance a store's personality and express its point of view.

So Gene Moore, who had had a brilliant career at Bonwit Teller, went on to greater heights at Tiffany's, where he has enjoyed complete freedom to express those artistic and innovative talents which have made him the foremost artist in the country in this most interesting field.

Walter Hoving
Chairman of the Board
Tiffany & Co.

W O R D S

As Tiffany's resident magician of display, Gene Moore has brought excitement, beauty, and drama to Fifth Avenue for over thirty years.

His dazzling Tiffany windows have offered an arresting glimpse into self-contained, miniature worlds—Moore's own very personal worlds with their blend of glamour and tension, their unexpected, often outlandish, marriages of the rough and the polished, and their mood of paradox.

Gene Moore's visual twists, his placements of gems and precious metals in disjointed contexts, his at once poetic and abrupt shifts of scale and texture may vary according to his infinitely subtle humor from the air of Surrealism to the joy of Impressionism. The range of his flair and imagination have proved boundless.

It is fitting that the brilliant and delightful universe of New York's and the world's foremost genius of window display be preserved in this extraordinary book for all of us to enjoy.

Henry Platt
President
Tiffany & Co.

WINDOWS AT TIFFANY'S

by Judith Goldman

*I*t is a cool November evening. Fifty-seventh Street is empty. It is just eight o'clock, but the deep blue winter sky makes it feel closer to midnight. Gene Moore is standing at the corner of Fifty-seventh Street and Fifth, oblivious to the chill in the air, studying a window. He is staring at a boudoir doll. Her long legs curl like smoke beneath her. She wears satin slippers, a cape of peach-colored ostrich feathers, and a rhinestone choker. The clothes are as worn as her matted wig. Looking tired and tarnished, she slouches suggestively, an odd procuress in the window of Tiffany & Co.

A chorus of dolls stand behind her: a French pierrot, an emaciated Dutch doll of indeterminate sex, a Shirley Temple doll with a vacant grin, and a Spanish señorita dressed in lavish black silks. In front of them, in an even line, sit seven small white porcelain boxes, each shaped like a turkey. Gene Moore is installing his twenty-fourth set of mid-November windows for Tiffany & Co., only the second set to celebrate Thanksgiving. The Limoges turkeys are the merchandise; the dolls are the window's stars.

Saying nothing, Moore studies the window. His assistant, Ronald Smith, stands next to him, studying Moore. The wind has rumpled Moore's silver hair and wrapped his tie about his neck. He is jacketless, but even in a shabby sweater and tattered twenty-year-old sneakers Moore remains too naturally elegant to appear casual. He has the luxurious presence of the self-contained man. He stands in front of the window with the authority of an impresario. Still as a cat, he examines his window with the solemn face of a funnyman. It is a face that keeps secrets. His eyes dart, checking details. He smiles, then, noticing something, grimaces. One cannot tell what he is thinking—if the window is what he expected, if he is pleased or disappointed. Moore insists he does not discover how a window will look until he installs it, that he depends on chance, intuition, and last-minute changes. After two minutes, Moore decides the light's too hard, and, suggesting they try a lavender filter, he heads back into the store.

Inside, the first floor of Tiffany's is airless. Emptied for the night, the diamond cases have a stealthy aura suggesting vacant crypts; the other cases, filled with rings and gold chains, jade and coral necklaces, stationery, pearls, fountain pens, and the latest designs by Elsa Peretti and Angela Cummings, appear oddly unenticing. Merchandising transforms latent desire into need. By making objects appear essential and glamorous, it agitates desire and turns even casual shoppers covetous. Merchandising depends on buyers, and without their noisy movement, a veil of stale sleep covers the store. Dolls clustered on counters are the only sign of life.

Head up, chest out, Moore strides through the store. Moving with the unhesitating ease of a dancer, he defines the space around him. A lean man, five feet nine inches tall, he has just turned seventy, but looks younger. His oldest feature are his gray-green eyes. Studying the dolls, he rearranges them. "Oh, don't look at me like that," he tells a Japanese doll he has just moved. "You'll be happy here. You look fine." To another he explains, "I don't know where to put you, but I like you, you'll have to go somewhere." Moore has been conversing with inanimate objects since he was a child, and on a regular basis he still talks to dogs, cats, trees, stone statues, and stars. These are not conversations meant to be overheard. Tonight's conversation is between the dolls and Moore; he believes in their imaginary lives.

Moore roams from counter to counter. A Pilgrim doll in a white-collared black Puritan smock, black breeches, and a tall hat sits by himself. Stopping, Moore adjusts the angle of his gun: "God damn it...I don't want you hiding that gun. Ron McNamer spent six months carving its handle." Having reprimanded the doll, Moore announces, to no one in particular, "I love his El Greco legs."

When adjustments are completed, Moore and Ron Smith transfer each group from counter to window. Flanked by sixteen lights—eight baby spots and eight auto spots—each window is a tiny stage, three feet high by twenty-two inches deep; movable side frames can create widths

ranging from one inch to four and a half feet. Moore would like to work with circles, ovals, trapezoids, or whatever shape struck his fancy, but he can produce only squares or rectangles, and he feels cramped by the restriction. "I work in a small theater with tremendous limitations."

What Moore lacks in space, he makes up for with light. He considers lighting the crucial aspect of display. "I am always aware of light. Without light you can't see. Light creates color, shadows. There is no dimension without light. But you shouldn't see light, you should feel it." After four decades, lighting has become second nature to Moore; instinctively, he can get the results he wants. But tonight's windows pose problems. White lights give the white turkeys a bluish cast. Lavender filters soften the white light, but the more pressing problem is space. Moore wants the light to hit the dolls and to create depth, and he hasn't the room to do both. Standing on a ladder, straddling the window, Moore twists like a monkey as he works the lights. "It's a good thing I studied ballet. You have to be an acrobat to work here."

A half hour passes, and lighting remains a problem. Moore asks for "two pink autos and one ice-blue baby." He tries another combination. Neither works. He continues to adjust the lights. "Where are you when I need you?" (Feigning desperation, he asks for help from the late Jean Rosenthal, the lighting designer who was his mentor.) "She'd know what to do."

As each window is completed, Moore and Smith walk out to Fifty-seventh Street to inspect it. They barely speak: nods convey messages. They return, make changes. It is close to midnight when they finish. Moore appears tired and relieved, yet preoccupied, almost apprehensive. The windows have taken him by surprise. They have not turned out as he expected. "They're inspired by James Ensor's paintings, and who cares about James Ensor? There isn't an honest girl in the bunch. They're depraved and depressed like I am."

They are strange, unpretty dolls. Their cloth faces, pulled tight like stocking masks, give them the ageless aspect of cretins. Huddled together, the innocent playthings look loony and forbidding. Worn, ragged, overhandled, each has been the object of someone else's affection, and they charge the air with seamy suggestions of unknown past encounters. The psychological drama unfolding in Tiffany's windows will turn passing observers into fleeting voyeurs.

The windows jar expectations. The old dolls are a bizarre contrast to the pristine white turkeys, each a symbol of the good life Thanksgiving celebrates. Childhood relics, they suggest spiritual entrapment; grouped

together, isolated and dumb, they flirt with the dark side of the American dream. Checking his cynicism, Moore creates an upbeat mood by transforming one of the windows into a shooting gallery in which the white porcelain turkeys move along an industrial conveyor belt. Beneath them sprawls the Pilgrim doll; hardly a symbol of Puritan purpose, the exhausted, elegant hunter lies collapsed in an amusement park display.

*C*harles Gene Moore has for the last twenty-five years been responsible for the face Tiffany & Co. presents to the world. Every two weeks he creates a new set of windows: two on Fifth Avenue and three on Fifty-seventh Street. It is the corner windows at Fifty-seventh and Fifth that, according to Moore, draw crowds. Pedestrians, he explains, slow down at corners; otherwise, they tend to keep moving.

A modest man, Moore prefers to attribute the attraction of Tiffany's windows to a rule of pedestrian traffic or to their location at a world-famous corner. Few corners compare. Other famous corners—State and Madison in Chicago, Hollywood and Vine in Hollywood—have become flashy intersections. In London there's the corner of Bond Street and Piccadilly; in Paris, the elegant junction where the rue Royale meets the rue St. Honoré; in Rome there's the odd-angled corner where expensive traffic flows, like gold, from the Via Babuino into the Piazza di Spagna. But none is like Fifty-seventh and Fifth. When natives or tourists think about New York, a gossamer image of Central Park, hansom cabs, and the Plaza Hotel springs to mind. The Art Deco bank vault of Tiffany & Co., itself a landmark, stands at the southeast corner of Fifty-seventh Street and Fifth, and from there one catches enough of a glimpse of New York's glittering symbols to feel part of the dream the city promises. But Tiffany's location at a world-famous corner hasn't much to do with Moore's loyal following. Moore continually receives mail—advice, requests for jobs, thank-you notes, display suggestions—from fans across the country who regard his windows as one of the city's sights. Farther up or down the Avenue, his windows would be crowd stoppers.

To display diamonds, rubies, sapphires, porcelain, clocks and watches, Moore builds designs out of string, rope, seashells, pasta, sand,

and eggs. In most windows, Moore creates a perilous balance between the unlikely and the obvious; he contrasts splendid jewels with the homeliest materials: twine, dirt, brown wrapping paper. Many windows feature paintings, sculpture, and collages, but only by unknown artists. Artists who have a gallery, a market, or a following "don't," he says, "need my space." In the mid-1950s, when Moore was working for both Bonwit Teller and Tiffany's, he hired unknown painters Jasper Johns and Robert Rauschenberg to create props for his windows. "Moore noticed me before Leo Castelli did," Rauschenberg says, laughing. Jasper Johns first exhibited his paintings, among them *Flag on Orange Field* (1957), in the windows of Bonwit's. Johns chose the pictures and Moore hung them, turning each window into a spare art gallery with one painting and one well-dressed mannequin.

Like those inspired by James Ensor, many windows refer to past art. Moore has created windows after Botticelli, Vermeer, Rousseau, Fragonard. One Valentine's Day he spoofed Whistler with a handwritten note on Tiffany stationery: "My own Darling Mother, Your portrait is an enormous success! Will you be my Valentine? Your loving son, Jamie." Moore has floated the Tiffany diamond over a wire skull to recall the imagery of Georgia O'Keeffe, and he has hung found objects and merchandise on old slabs of wood so the viewer couldn't tell which was which, an homage to the nineteenth-century trompe l'oeil painter William Harnett. During World War II, when blackouts precluded spotlights, he created windows after Vermeer at Bonwit Teller: "They were perfect, because in a Vermeer, light comes through one window. I used a flashlight, built interiors after Vermeer, and dressed mannequins in Pauline Trigère's velvet at-home clothes inspired by Vermeer."

Purveying good taste by avoiding its look, Moore escapes the arid elegance that can accompany "good design," punctuating his spare compositions with surprising sentiments and intentional mistakes. If eight perfectly even rows of knives are facing left, one knife faces right. A window of small white eggs includes one brown egg. Moore began disrupting his own symmetry to test audience attention. But the test was soon a trademark: the planned irregularity became a regular occurrence, a way to add drama and invite participation.

The simplicity central to Moore's style (like its source—nature) can be gentle or unruly and is almost always unpredictable. Natural materials—seashells, sand, real grass, dirt, birds, nests, eggs, leaves, and swamps—appear in windows as often as diamonds, but never the same way twice; and although themes dictated by seasons and holidays seldom

No! No! No! this is not precious city water.
It's just some unprecious old gin.

vary, the windows are never the same. Christmas brings champagne, Santa, angels, snow, cathedrals, and skiing accidents. February means love's traumas, hearts, flowers, and retreats from winter—seashore fantasies of shells, sand, and fishing trips. Easter windows sport eggs, bunnies, real grass, fresh lilies, and birds' nests. Summer is heralded by flag-waving, lemonade, crossword puzzles, and lawn mowers. Butterflies, a Moore staple, appear in every season.

Every window is different, but every window, one way or another, manages to suggest that all's right with the world, and that if it's not, it soon will be. Moore has the heart of a cornball and the mind of a fish-eyed cynic. Forever giving his audience errant glimpses of hard luck and bad times, he leaves them smiling. In a Moore window, Easter eggs break, grass grows wild, hearts shatter, and the buried victim of a skiing accident holds, in her extended hand, a crystal champagne glass. Moore is an optimist by default, not design.

Seldom what they seem, Moore's windows when obvious, are also oblique; if comic, they're serious. When they look simple, they can be as complicated as the doll windows, which relied on layers of contrast between an unspeakable sophistication and innocence, between sloth and Puritanism, between the industrial hardware of a conveyor belt and the porcelain knickknacks one expects to find on a well-dressed table.

Moore's windows are always well-informed. During the 1978 newspaper strike, Moore complained that he was miserable working without information. Mirrors of metropolitan activity, his windows reflect what goes on in the city. They have celebrated the opening of the opera, the ballet, a Picasso exhibition, and a Philharmonic season. To protest the childishness of the 1963 newspaper strike, Moore papered the background of the windows with sheets of New York papers, and to emphasize the point he included toys—a model train and blocks—covered with newsprint. During a transit workers' strike, his windows showed alternate forms of transportation: pogo sticks, roller skates, a unicycle. Not above politics, and addicted to puns, Moore placed a black quill—a stand-in for the head of the Transport Workers' Union—under the wheel of an exercise machine. (Mike Quill died a few days later.)

During a summer water shortage, gushing fountains appeared in the windows along with a calligraphed explanation that the spouting liquid was not water but gin. Soon after the window's installation, a fire marshal appeared with a summons; the New York City Fire Department regarded gin, an inflammable liquid, as a hazard. Indignant (he resents interference of any kind), Moore climbed into the window and struck a match. Nothing exploded, and the protesting inspector left with his summons in his hand.

One week Moore's windows may be topical and reportorial; two weeks later they may be irreverent, whimsical, or sentimental. Moore runs a street theater with a broad and unpredictable repertoire. He has presented the story of a jewel heist perpetrated by an earnest gray mouse. He has built compositions with architectural fragments of a changing New York. In elegant still lifes combining completed tax forms with aspirin bottles, pencils, red tape, a classified telephone directory open to

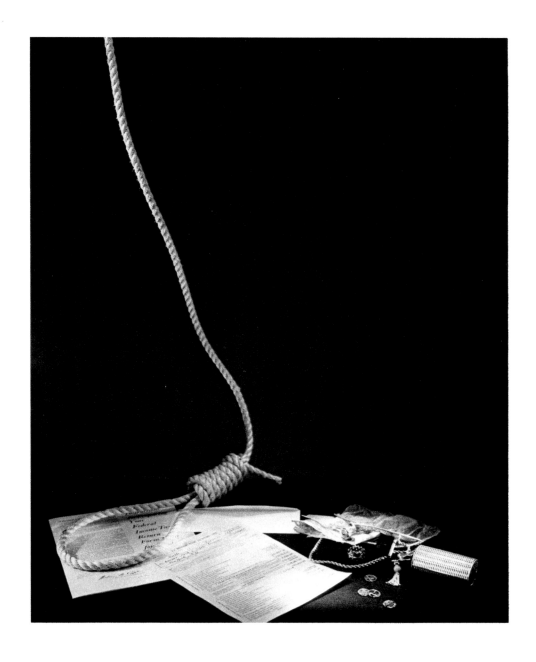

pawnshop listings, a noose, and a pistol he has dramatized the financial troubles of various New Yorkers as reflected by their income-tax forms. Suicide is contemplated by one New York resident, who lists her occupation as taxpayer, resides at the geographically impossible "corner of Park and Fifth Avenue," and owes the IRS $180,071.18. At least once a month the windows feature a production concerning romantic distress or bliss: two china rhinoceroses touch ungainly noses to proclaim love's fragile balance; "Love you" is spelled out in gumdrops; "Amor" is constructed of sugar cubes. Love, after all, is an emotion on which Tiffany & Co. tries to corner the market.

Bonwit Teller, December 2, 1949. Artist, Jac Venza

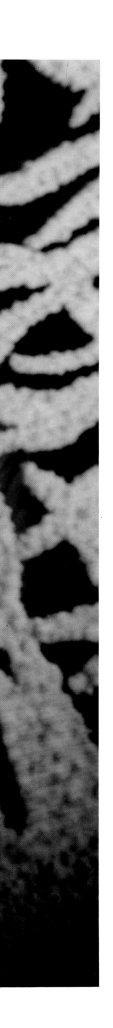

Bonwit Teller, December 2, 1949. Artist, Jac Venza

The miniature dramas tell timeworn stories—about crime, punishment, death, love, and taxes. In every window, the audience discovers something they've never thought of or something they've always known. Moore gives old sentiments a new context. Surprise is his mainstay. One does not expect to see a jewel robbery acted out in the windows of a jewelry store.

*I*n the trade, people who have worked with Moore—display manufacturers, photographers, artists, fashion editors, dress designers, and architects—have an awesome respect for him. They describe him as brilliant and professional and say he is a gentle man and a genius.

"When he put a diamond on a piece of lettuce, he invented a new way to present jewels," says Pauline Trigère. "One never knows what he'll do. He could make a carrot glamorous. Every designer owes something to Gene. He opened display to art. Whenever I see what he's done, I jump for joy and marvel at his talent."

"I have always had complete confidence in his taste and aesthetic sense," says Walter Hoving, chairman of the board of Tiffany & Co.

"I wouldn't tell Fellini what to do, and I wouldn't tell Gene," says Gino DiGrandi, a barrel-chested Brooklyn-born Italian impresario who organizes exhibitions and sales campaigns for industries and governments and was once the husband of Italian film director Lina Wertmuller. Di-Grandi has worked with Moore on various projects, from promotions for pasta to promotions for women's wigs. "Moore knows he must sell," says DiGrandi, "but he takes that reality and turns it into fantasy; he makes the normal superb. Talking to him an enormous synthesis occurs; it is better than a quart of Scotch. Moore has given art form to window dressing. He is a genius."

When the word genius is mentioned, Moore bristles. "The word genius is like love, misused and overused. Albert Einstein was a genius. Thornton Wilder was a genius. A genius is someone who goes beyond everything. It is when God has his right hand on your shoulder. I am not a genius, I'm just a window trimmer."

Although Moore tries to avoid discussions about his career and his talent, he is not unaware of his success. He receives compliments with the casual assurance of someone who knows they're deserved. It is when praise turns excessive (and Moore considers anything besides a simple "Well done" excessive) that he describes himself as "just a window trimmer." The statement, delivered frequently and with an emphatic self-deprecatory shrug, means, "What is the fuss about? It's just a window, not a symphony, a sonata, a ballet, or a painting." Moore does not consider his windows Art with a capital A—a notion he finds pretentious—and he does not think of himself as an artist.

Moore holds art in high regard. An aesthetic conservative, he believes there is a difference between high art and low art, between fine art and applied art. Fine art needs no qualifiers. Created in a no-man's-land where no boundaries exist, art has no rules. The applied arts (variously termed commercial art, decorative art, functional art, architectural design, or simply design) are worldly products, made to meet a variety of specifications, deadlines, requirements, and personal preferences. Art has no function; the applied arts must work. A great poster must graphically broadcast an event; a toaster, no matter how brilliantly conceived and executed, must brown the bread. A window design can charm, cajole, amuse, seduce, illuminate, entertain. It can lift the spirits, but if merchandise doesn't move, according to Moore, the window fails.

Windows, however, have long been a subject of art. Vermeer knew what to do with a window. To Vermeer, windows were a source of light,

Bonwit Teller, April 19, 1959

dimension, texture, and composition. One looks into a Vermeer, as
through a window, at an interior still life. Atget's photographs of Paris
shopwindows, which show the reflection of the windows' observers, give
viewers immediate access to Paris streets. By his angle or distance,
Walker Evans framed American storefronts into abstract still lifes. Moore
sometimes smiles enigmatically when talk turns to art, for though the object of his windows is merchandising, the subject is invariably art. Art is
Moore's main source. Forever an art student, he has studied windows on
museum walls as he has seashells (when Moore thinks of seashells, he

remembers a whole week spent at the Uffizi looking at Botticelli's "Venus on the Half Shell"). Art is also Moore's secret metaphor. His windows create the illusion of art. He makes Tiffany's heavy stainless steel frames act as literal frames for his compositions, and when windows feature narrative dramas, he transforms each frame into a proscenium arch. Moore uses light to create depth, size to create scale, and mirrors (which appeared more regularly at Bonwit Teller) to remind viewers that window gazing is an act of reflection. Moore employs the look of art to engage his audience and lead them through the thoughtful compositions—past the butterflies and eggs and real grass—to the crystal, porcelain, and jewels.

*I*n its own time, commercial art seldom receives serious attention. There is a prejudice against art that functions and art that sells, and that prejudice, a peculiarly American bias, reflects our uneasy feelings toward art. Art suggests regal pleasures and reveals undemocratic advantages. Talent, which forms its own aristocracy, proves that all men are not created equal. We find art most palatable if kept pure, less threatening if viewed out of the context of its marketplace, audience, or function. This prejudice is so entrenched that arguments continue on whether the crafts (ceramics, glass, et al.) deserve the designation art. (Craft implies work, not inspiration.) Even the images of Pop art in the late fifties and the sixties outraged critics: they deplored an art that took inspiration and borrowed icons from the landscape of an industrial society. To use an ale can or Brillo box as art's subject matter was to debase art with a commercial connection.

The applied arts are ignored or deemed only fashion until time gives their worldly taint the patina of respectability or—as happened in the late seventies—until a drought strikes the land of high art and a mannerist stretch sets in. Then the other arts are rediscovered, reexamined, and, usually with great fanfare, made the subjects of books and museum exhibitions. One notable attempt to connect the applied and fine arts was made in 1949 by the Museum of Modern Art. The exhibition "Modern Art in Your Life," directed by Robert Goldwater and René d'Harnoncourt, showed the relation between skyscrapers and Mondrian's *Broadway Boogie Woogie* (1942–43), between Léger and commercial graphics. between Sur-

Bonwit Teller, May 14, 1957. Artist, Jordan Steckel

realism and shopwindows. (The exhibition included two of Moore's windows.)

But the distinction between fine and commercial art grows hard to make. Art has become a magic merchandising word, and it is currently used to describe everything from limited edition bedsheets to Detroit cars. More and more, today's museums function like merchandising marts, and department store interiors have been broken up into series of boutiques that simulate the special atmosphere once characteristic of art galleries. Meanwhile, art galleries, always merchandising marts of sorts, appear more aggressively commercial. Taste has been homogenized by the speed at which print and TV convey information, and art quickly gets watered down, reduced to a common denominator. What appears on canvas one week may decorate towels and shower curtains a month later, and vice versa. Even shopwindows have a sameness about them.

Fifteen years ago, before the whole world went groovy, a store's windows proclaimed its philosophy. Fifteen years ago, every Fifth Avenue shopper knew that Lord & Taylor was a store for ladies, that Bonwit Teller catered to more sophisticated types, that country types preferred Peck & Peck, and that women who liked looking ahead of their time could find Space Age accouterments at Henri Bendel.

Merchandising has changed. The crowded interior displays and the confusing abundance of merchandise now found in many better shops appear to be an intentional recreation of the hurly-burly atmosphere of the discount store. Fragmented layouts not only suggest the exclusive bou-

tique; presented one on top of another, they imitate the natural, haphazard order of a real city. The effect on shoppers is a physical and psychological disorientation. Only a purchase affords a shopper relief from the chaos; an acquisition provides a focus—an object or place to call one's own.

This merchandising method has grown so prevalent that it is hard to distinguish stores from one another. They feature identical merchandise and employ similar sales techniques, and their windows reflect this. Windows no longer have a distinct look. Only dime-store windows, showing the objects we need, and the windows at Tiffany & Co., displaying the objects we want, still announce their intentions.

The sameness of windows disturbs Moore, and he's convinced merchandising has taken a turn for the worse. He thinks it's because "everyone's a zombie, running fast. People walk around in a semiconscious state; they don't have the slightest idea they're being insulted or assaulted. No one has time. I think the world's probably coming to an end, and I'm glad I won't be around to see it." Ask Moore if he sees a parallel between current art and merchandising, and he says, faking a playful impatience, "So what else is new?" But ask if he sees a connection between the common, everyday objects the Pop artists made famous and his own use of string, rope, eggs, and it is obvious that his patience is really being tested: "That is a dumb question. I'm not Andy Warhol; I'm Gene Moore; I am a designing window trimmer and a window trimming designer, and I'm unhappy if I don't have an idea."

Moore has ideas all the time: on the Seventy-second Street cross-

31

town bus, which he rides to work every morning; at his country house in New Jersey, where he gardens; in conversations with his tiger cat, Daki. Moore assumes everyone has an imagination as unbridled as his own, and people who ask him "How did you ever think of that?" amaze him. Some-one tells him a dream and it becomes the basis of a window. For Moore there is no gap between his work and his life. Everything he sees and hears affects him: children eating ice-cream cones or playing hopscotch, the shapes of pasta, the color of gumdrops. Moore has never made a sketch for a window; he visualizes what he will do, accumulates material, and usually improvises the drama or design once he's climbed into the window.

Gene Moore does not like to discuss his childhood. He does not believe in the past and has a hard time remem-bering what he did the day before yesterday. His sense of privacy is matched by courtly Southern manners, which sometimes cause him inad-vertently to reveal things he hadn't meant to at all. When his guard drops and he does tell stories on himself, he is genuinely surprised, and when listeners show interest he grows uncomfortable and his eyes open wide, becoming large and as insistent as stop signs. If conversations turn per-sonal, Moore changes the subject. He discusses trips to Italy to study paintings; the first time he heard Stravinsky's music; the costumes and sets he designed for Sir John Gielgud. At different times in his life he has studied ballet, piano, painting, and on most subjects he has a cultivated opinion. When actually questioned about his past, Moore playfully answers questions with questions: "If you live in the South, what are you going to get interested in, kicking a football and being a high school hero?"

"Everyone loves Gene," says one old friend, "but no one knows him. He keeps to himself. The opening of an envelope is not for Gene Moore." Another friend, Jim Buckley, who over thirty years ago gave Moore his first job in display, says, "It's hard to get a fix on his personality." Moore appears aloof. He holds his head at a slight upward tilt, and as he is usually thinking about at least three things at once, he often appears distracted. His guard, meticulous, well-mannered, practiced, is sometimes mistaken for the cultivated poise of a snob. This upsets Moore, who gleefully admits to an array of snobberies about food, theater, art, movies, ballet, and fashion, "but not," he says, "about people. No one ever realizes that I'm shy."

At one time, Moore regarded his shyness as a disease. "When I was in my early thirties, I was so easily intimidated by people that I couldn't talk. I was scared to call the phone company. It held me back. Being in business meant being an actor, and I couldn't act. One night, lying in bed, I decided that if I deliberately put myself in the most embarrassing situation in the world and lived through it, I could overcome my shyness. It was crazy reasoning, but the next morning I enrolled in a beginners' class at the School of American Ballet."

Born in Birmingham, Alabama, on June 10, 1910, Moore was the youngest of three boys. He never lived with his family ("I was shipped around hither and yon"), and his earliest memory of the South is the desire to leave it. The place he remembers was provincial, segregated, a home where he was never at home. He remembers feeling like an outsider, getting along better with Southern blacks than Southern whites, time spent reading, drawing, and taking dolls and toy cars apart. He remembers going to movies, practicing piano, hating mathematics "because math was like football, it meant learning rules." When he was twelve, he wanted to be a concert pianist. Soon after, he recalls seeing Mary Roberts Rinehart's melodrama *The Cat and the Canary* and from then on being a fan. He attended every theatrical and dance production that came to Birmingham. He saw the Ballets Russes, the Ziegfeld Follies, Ruth St. Denis and Ted Shawn. He remembers filling a scrapbook with stage and screen memorabilia, subscribing to *Photoplay Magazine*, and spending whatever time he could at the Alabama Theatre, watching movies.

"Every Saturday I'd escape to the movies. I hated my Southern accent; I learned to speak at the movies. I'd sit through them twice, then I'd practice and practice. One day a teacher drawled, 'Who are you trying to kid?' But I kept going anyway. I knew I'd get out of the South some day. Movies were new. They were modern. I was in awe of Lillian Gish and Gloria Swanson. I believed there was a life like that. I became aware of presence, of how it affected glamour. Glamour became a reality to me."

After high school, Moore sold shoes at the College Slipper Shop, and in 1929 he left Birmingham to study painting at the Chicago Academy of Fine Arts. "It was the depression. I was lonely and broke and I spent my Sundays at the Art Institute." A year later, he returned to Birmingham, where he spent the next five years trying to get to New York. He painted portraits, worked in an ice-cream factory and as an usher at the Alabama Theatre, taught blacks on relief to paint children's stuffed toys.

In 1935, Moore arrived in New York with fourteen dollars, the ambition to paint, and a self-imposed ultimatum. "I said, 'Charley, you have five years to make a go of it, or else you have to return to the South.' " (Moore does not know how he came to be called by his middle name, Gene; in all conversations with himself he answers to Charley.)

Moore says he was born the year he came to New York. "I was a case of arrested development. I never had roots until I came to New York; life, my life, didn't begin until then. I arrived in the afternoon and I walked all night. I read newspapers looking for jobs. There were none. I was exhausted. I didn't know anyone. I was leaning against one of the lions in front of the New York Public Library, the one whose nose points down Forty-first Street. I had to talk to someone, so I asked the lion what I should do. As soon as I started talking to the lion, I felt my roots going down. He said, 'Follow my nose.' I did. At the time, I didn't know he was a copy of the lion in Trafalgar Square." The lion's nose led Moore to Morehouse–Barlow, a religious bookstore on Forty-first Street, where for the next eight months he swept floors, emptied wastebaskets, and dusted books.

In the last forty years, the display field has changed. Today's schools of commercial art offer courses in Visual Merchandising, and window trimmers are called Visual Merchandisers or Display Directors. One does not grow up wanting to be a window trimmer, and Moore's career in display was not part of his plan. When he entered the field, display was considered the bottom rung of merchandising. Schools did not teach the elements of display, and the field was not what today might be called a Career Alternative. But it was a field that offered safe harbor and modest incomes to people with talent and artistic ambitions who wanted to be something else, to be painters or sculptors, dancers or actors, cartoonists or illustrators.

Early in their careers, many artists once labeled Pop supported themselves with jobs in display: not only Jasper Johns and Robert Rauschenberg, but James Rosenquist and Andy Warhol. All four worked

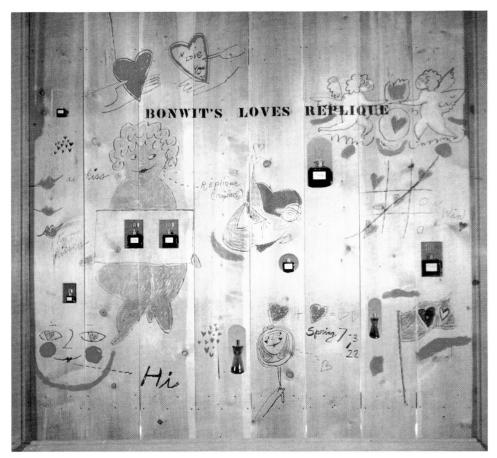

Bonwit Teller, July 4, 1955. Wood fence decorated by Andy Warhol

for Moore. Before he wrote *The Wonderful Wizard of Oz,* L. Frank Baum
had been a traveling salesman, a shopkeeper, a window trimmer, and editor of *The Shop Window: A Journal of Window Trimming,* the first magazine on display (1897–1903). Baum created the magazine because no other
work left him time to write, and editing at home did. Maurice Sendak got
his start working in display at F.A.O. Schwarz: the toy store's book
buyer, impressed by his sketches and the imaginary creatures he made
for windows, introduced him to an editor at Harper & Row. Playwright
Herb Gardner, author of *A Thousand Clowns,* worked for display com-
panies, making miniature replicas of nineteenth-century Newark and
Nativity scenes, for a two-year period that ended the Christmas he grew
bored and was fired for turning out cross-eyed Wise Men.

Before he designed the Twentieth Century Limited, the Greyhound
bus, and machinery for International Harvester, Raymond Loewy worked
in display at Macy's and Saks Fifth Avenue. In the early twenties Norman
Bel Geddes was display director of Franklin Simon. Architect and sculptor
Frederick Kiesler also designed shopwindows, and in his 1930 theoretical
text on display, *Contemporary Art Applied to the Store and Its Display,* he
aptly described the displayman:

"[He] must be young in spirit and agile.... [He] must always be on

37

Model for stage set, *The Ides of March,* 1963

the qui vive. He is the first to read dozens of periodicals, he overlooks no important theater opening, he neglects no important film or exhibition. He must be able to absorb information like a sponge. There must be no limit to his capacity for knowledge.

"He is a silent market crier. His ancestors squatted in marketplaces, lounged in the doorways of ghetto streets, sprang about on the platform of a circus outfit. 'This way, gentlemen! Here, only here can you see....' All this he does, but in a refined, subtle, invisible, inaudible way."

The difference between Moore and the illustrious company that has passed through display is that Moore has remained in the field. However, he has created designs for many things besides windows: packages for vitamins and perfumes; sets and costumes for the Equity Library Theatre's production of *Pal Joey* (1948); sets for Stage 73's production of García Lorca's *If Five Years Pass* (1962); sets and costumes for John Gielgud's production of *The Ides of March* (1963); costumes for the Glen Tetley Dance Company (1968–69). From 1966 to 1973, Moore, as Tiffany's head of design development for gold jewelry, created brooches, rings, compacts, and cuff links as well as windows. His first design, a safety pin set with pavé diamonds, was a huge success. ("I saw a safety pin lying on the

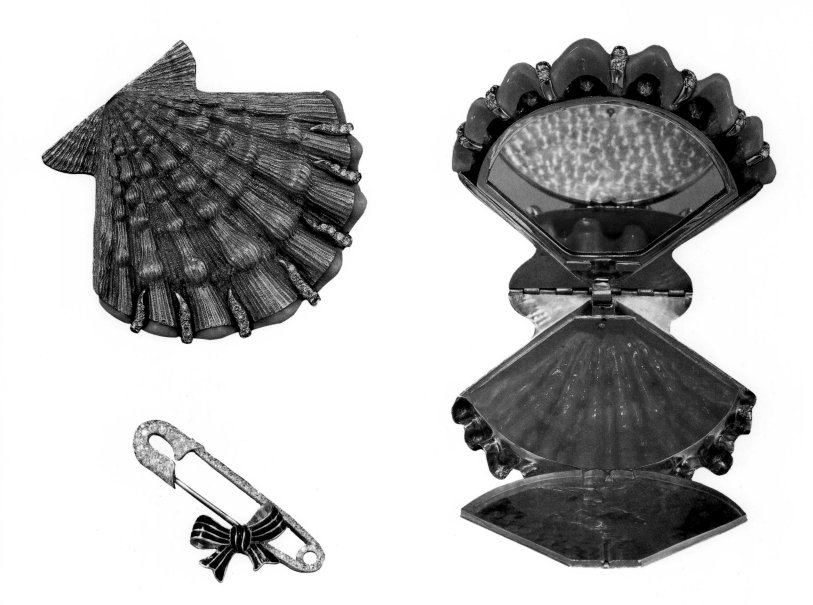

floor one morning, and I thought, what a pretty, practical shape.") In the early 1970s, Moore created an opulent-looking pillbox set with forty-seven garnets and one bright diamond, reintroducing garnets because he foresaw the return of Victorian taste. Moore has designed rings inspired by owls, Egyptian motifs, a square hardware-store bolt; cuff links and lighters; elaborate brooches set with unusual semiprecious stones; and a Noah's ark of jeweled and enameled animals—among them a whimsical giraffe with emerald eyes, a lion with a diamond mane, and a bashful deer with diamond antlers. Moore has never designed a cat. "I could create a dog without whiskers, but what's a cat without whiskers? And how could I ever translate those little chin hairs into gold?"

Lion's-paw shell compact, 1969. Gold
with diamonds (Hanns Krahmer)

Safety pin, 1967. Gold, set with pavé
diamonds (Carvin French Jewelers)

Horse, deer, zebra, tiger, giraffe,
lion, 1968–69. Gold, enamel, and
diamonds (Hanns Krahmer)

Pillbox, 1971. Gold set with garnets
and a diamond (Falai of Florence)

During the period in the late 1950s when Moore was working simultaneously for Bonwit Teller and Tiffany's, every two weeks he produced
twenty-seven windows which wrapped around half a square city block.
He also conceived the violet motif that became Bonwit Teller's trademark. "They wanted a ladylike, sophisticated image; I brought in a violet-
patterned Victorian teacup I had at home and said, 'This is it.' " In 1959,
long before women began wearing nightgowns to garden parties, Moore
designed feminine nightwear that looked like formal gowns. He also
produced the first line of laughing mannequins. Patterned after real-life
people, his look-alikes for Rosalind Russell, Audrey Hepburn, Vivien
Leigh, and models Suzy Parker and Sunny Harnett had broad, toothy

grins. (Until then, mannequins wore haughty, enigmatic looks.) At the time, people considered the Sunny Harnett model shocking, for she was not only laughing but lying down.

Moore has also designed films, installations for the Museum of Modern Art and for world's fairs, airplane interiors, photographic sets, and fashion shows. From 1947 to 1957, when he had an after-hours career going as a photographer, Moore took pictures of Audrey Hepburn, Gloria Vanderbilt, Suzy Parker, and most of the talent under contract to the late

Bonwit Teller, 1953. Rosalind Russell making a midnight appearance in honor of the debut of her look-alike mannequin

Sol Hurok. Moore rejects as many jobs as he accepts. Some years ago, he turned down a six-figure job with Revlon because they wouldn't guarantee him aesthetic control, and he stopped working for Condé Nast after they reduced his photographs for a perfume layout to postage-stamp size.

Over the years, Moore has received a great deal of press coverage, and he keeps his clippings in three large dog-eared scrapbooks. He attracts odd headlines. "Sado-Masochism Hits Home Furnishings" appeared (when innocence still had an audience) to describe windows for Clarence House in which he showed leathers for upholstery, a motorcycle, its rider, chains, and a pink rose about to be crushed under the bike's wheel. "Hare-brained Rabbits in Bonwit's the Result of Serious Thought" reports on a window of rabbits and accessories and calls Moore the "brains behind the bunnies." The clippings amuse Moore. They also amaze him, for until he sees them, he seldom remembers what he's done. "I do things that interest me, and when I finish I do something else."

For projects and people he considers special, Moore has an excellent memory. He precisely remembers first meeting Irene Worth, seeing her in a lemon-yellow Chanel suit across the Elgin Marbles room of the British Museum. He can describe in detail the costumes he regularly designs for the dance company of his friend Paul Taylor, or his installation of Joseph Cornell's collage boxes at the Leo Castelli Gallery, in which he created an atmosphere that matched the audible silence of a Cornell box. He takes civic pride in having created a New York landmark and a national fashion when he lit the Seagram Building Christmas trees with tiny white bulbs. Moore felt honored and impressed when he was invited to design the dinner party that President and Mrs. Kennedy gave at Mount Vernon for the President of Pakistan. He does not remember the journalistic fuss the expensive party caused, but he does remember the natural glow he created on the trees lining Mount Vernon's driveway, the full-dress Marines flanking the road, the Fife and Drum Corps in eighteenth-century costumes, the flowers from Mrs. Paul Mellon's gardens, the platform for the symphony orchestra—and the mosquitoes. Moore insisted on a dress rehearsal, and he made them spray for mosquitoes; he didn't attend the party because "everything was perfect, I wasn't needed."

But the drama of a presidential dinner or a theatrical commission does not detour Moore. Whatever else he does, he returns to his windows. He says his art form is window trimming. "The problem with theater is, too many people have too much to say. In a window, you write the script, set the stage, and direct the production. I can take pressure, but I can't take a lot of people yapping at me."

Scene from "Dust," June 1, 1977. Choreography by Paul Taylor, set and costumes by Gene Moore

Moore's favorite word is kismet, and although he gives equal credence to hard work and to luck, he believes above all in chance. Moore talks about "being in the right place at the right time," and punctuates his sophisticated conversation with fatalistic dicta like "If your number's up, your number's up" and "If someone wants to pull your strings, your strings get pulled." Yet last spring when he slipped in the kitchen and cracked a vertebra, Moore was convinced he'd done something to deserve it. He is a moonwatcher who blames mishaps and delays on the shape of the moon, and he is so persuaded that being a Gemini makes a difference that he feels inordinately secure when working

with other Geminis. To date, all his assistants at Tiffany's have been named Ronald, and while Moore does not know what that means, he is sure it means something. Although not religious, Moore regularly goes to St. Patrick's to light candles for friends who need help. He believes that fate plays a large role in all decisions, from small ones ("Everything anyone does or says, the decisions they make, depends a great deal on what they had for breakfast") to big ones like his career in display.

Like other young painters, when he first came to New York Moore took whatever jobs he could find. After the bookstore, he worked as a waiter on a South American cruise ship, as a scenic assistant at a Berkshire summer theater, at the Bois Smith Display Company making papier-mâché flowers. It was while he was at Bois Smith that he met Jim Buckley, then a freelance window designer. Buckley, who was working on a display called "Hounds of Spring," had ordered wire-mesh dogs, to be covered with different-colored leaves, and Moore made the dogs. Buckley remembers him as "shy, artistic, diligent, respectful. He had a quick, sardonic wit; he looked askance at all phoniness, and so did I." In 1937, when I. Miller hired Buckley as its display director, Buckley hired Moore as his assistant.

In the late 1930s, Surrealism was in the air. A World War was beginning. Artists talked about dreams, nightmares, the subconscious, and made art out of disparate, violent images. Some artists, like André Breton, Marcel Duchamp, Salvador Dali, used shopwindows as their arena. The windows Salvador Dali designed for Bonwit Teller in 1939, which put him on the artistic map, also had a lasting effect on display. In the window that he says "did more for my glory than if I'd eaten up all of Fifth Avenue," Dali covered walls with shocking-pink satin, stuck them with hand mirrors, filled a Persian-lamb–lined bathtub with water and narcissus. Out of the tub rose disembodied hands, each holding a hand mirror that flashed a reflection of a mannequin wrapped in coq feathers. Her face was bloody and bugs crawled through her long hair.

Shopwindows offer grand, fanciful self-reflections. Merchandise is displayed as dreams money can buy, dreams that promise adventure, romance, and fulfillment. By turning private pleasures menacing in a public tableau, Dali gave the dreams meant to entice shoppers aspects of a nightmare. Narcissism, not need, he implied, was the shopper's motivation; blood and bugs were the punishment for the sin of self-love.

Buckley's Surrealism was gentle compared to that of the European painters. But if less of an exhibitionist than Dali, Buckley was as much of a showman, and his windows for I. Miller and later for Bergdorf Goodman attracted a large following. Before Buckley's regime, Bergdorf's windows had featured headless forms in couture clothes. Buckley's displays, in comparison, were radical. In windows on a musical theme, Buckley positioned mannequins as randomly as notes on a page of music: one rose from a piano, another dangled in midair, plucking the piano's strings; a hanging basket sported a glove; merchandise—shoes and hats—was strewn everywhere. Sheet music formed the mannequins' heads, arms, and legs, and each wore a flowing, rhythmic gown. To those who would acquire the fashions on display, the daft spectacle promised lyric rapture.

"When I met Buckley, I still wanted to be a painter. But I had begun to realize I wasn't going to be great. It's hard to admit you can't be best. But I didn't want to be a painter if I wasn't going to be a very good one. Working with Buckley I became serious about display. He was brilliant. He had such fantasy in his mind—this all-knowing, all-seeing knowledge. He was interested in everything, and I became interested in everything. People think you can study display. Schools teach it. But the only way to study display is to study everything else. Art, music, dance, literature. Display is about awareness; it is about keeping your eyes and ears open."

Moore takes every opportunity to credit Buckley as the major influence on his career—along with the music of Mozart, Debussy, Stravinsky; the scenic designs of Edward Gordon Craig; the writings of William Shakespeare, Colette, Willa Cather, Anaïs Nin, Isak Dinesen; ballet; wildflowers; animals (particularly cats); and the shapes and colors of dimestore merchandise. Buckley says Moore gives him too much credit. "Every five or ten years we meet, and after we celebrate meeting, Gene thanks me for inspiring his success. But Gene was always an original. As soon as he began working at Delman's, windows became his stage."

At Delman's, where Moore worked from 1938 to 1945, every window featured fourteen pairs of shoes and as many matching handbags. "It could get tedious. All those shoes, and buyers yapping, wanting to put more shoes in the window, never realizing that accessories, because they're so small, are hard items to display. But the merchandise doesn't matter; what sells is how you show it." At Delman's Moore hung shoes from strings (then a radical idea); piled hundreds in heaps and placed a bewildered-looking mannequin in the middle of the disarray; filled baby carriages with shoes and spring flowers.

Delman's was part of Bergdorf Goodman, and Bergdorf's embodied the glamour Moore grew up on at the movies. Seldom given to nostalgia, Moore sounds wistful when he talks about "Papa Goodman, who loved furs and beautiful women" or "Mr. Delman, who left me alone." "That

was when there was such a thing as an expensive store, when there was a grandeur to merchandising. Before there were Paris copies, when a gown from Paris meant an original. Women were beautiful then, and Bergdorf's was the store of the world's most expensively kept women."

*M*oore's interest in fashion developed at Bonwit Teller, where he filled twenty-two windows every week with furs, swimwear, lingerie, handbags, gloves, and back-to-school clothes. To get the merchandise he wanted, Moore had to know fashion, and from 1945 to 1961 he steeped himself in it. He followed the Paris collections, watched Seventh Avenue, and spent hours, he says, turning clothes inside out to see how they were made.

Moore has been interested in fashion ever since, and every day at noon when he walks from Tiffany's to Larre's, a restaurant on Fifty-sixth Street where he has lunched for the last thirty years, he takes in the passing parade. Nowadays he finds the walk depressing. Current fashion disheartens him. He dislikes what are called fun furs, blue jeans in the city, and boots (except for inclement weather), and he finds sloppy the look called "layered." "Today everything's called innovative and nothing's new. Most of today's expensive casual fashions are derivative, particularly of Claire McCardell and Bonnie Cashin."

A good design, according to Moore, makes women look beautiful and feminine; he deplores the fact that women no longer look like ladies. He admires Pauline Trigère and Galanos because both create elegant, structured, original clothes, Stavropoulos because he makes clothes full of glamour. His measure for great American design is the late Norman Norell, with whom he thinks fewer than a handful of designers can compare.

Moore's opinions about fashion do not waver. "I always know when something's right and I know when it's wrong." Moore and Norell became friends when, with a gesture of characteristic arrogance, Moore removed a pink rose from the sash of a white satin Norell gown he showed in Bonwit's window. The day after the gown appeared, Norell called to find out what had happened to his rose. "I told him I'd taken it off, that it ruined an otherwise brilliant design. He said, 'OK' and hung up."

The disappearance of quality, good grooming, and ladies is a favorite

Bonwit Teller, October 17, 1961

topic, and it comes up so often in Moore's conversation that he can sound like an antiquated Edwardian. But he is a man who believes taste and style reflect how we live, who we are, and what we think of ourselves. To Moore, good grooming means more than well-polished shoes, hemlines without safety pins, stockings without runs; good grooming reflects a state of self-respect, and Moore finds its current absence symptomatic of a more general malaise. To Moore the disordered look of current fashion mirrors a society on the outs with itself, a society that no longer values work quality or individuality. It is not the decline of fashion that disturbs Moore but the decline of style. Style has authority and reflects individuality; fashion does not. Fashion is a mass taste bearing a price tag, and Moore turns wide-eyed with bewilderment at the prices paid for clothing he finds shabby and unflattering.

Bonwit's windows became famous. Figurative counterparts to the three-dimensional abstractions Moore now creates for Tiffany's, they engaged viewers with elaborate narratives, spare designs, and romantic promises and surprised them with unexpected images and implications that in the 1950s seemed risqué. Their key elements were fantasy, humor, and the unexpected, and the public reaction to them was "Ah!"— Moore's favorite response to a window. "Ah!" translates to "But of course!" and means a window has made its point.

In a set of back-to-school windows, Moore filled the space with books. A physiology book was open to an illustration of female genitalia. A

50

Bonwit Teller, May 16, 1961

few days later, the store received a complaint calling the display obscene and Moore closed the book, delighted that his window had been read and had garnered its "Ah!" In another Bonwit display, mannequins in expensive, tailored suits stood under scaffolds holding buckets of dripping paint. The suggestion of the clothes' possible ruin gave them value; the suggestion that the ladies would escape the falling paint implied that good clothes act as an amulet in messy situations. In those days, fashion promised a charmed life.

In the late 1970s, similar windows appeared, but the paint was no longer about to spill; it drenched the mannequins. Disaster did not hover in the wings; it had struck. For a while, every imaginable indignity took place in shopwindows. Fashion no longer meant safety from the ravages of time and chance; fashion brought conflict and confusion. Lacking fantasy and devoid of style, to Moore the masochism was trumped up, the trendy, flip side of the prevailing narcissism and one more sign of the disintegration of taste. Moore disliked it and discounted the windows. "They won't sell. A shocking scene can stop viewers, but it can't engage them."

Explanations flourished for what was briefly called sado-masochistic chic. Some said the coupling of the decadent and disastrous to sell taste and fashion reflected the sentiments of the new woman: her ambivalent attitudes toward fashion and old sex roles. But to Moore all explanations—including the much-bandied-about journalistic dictum that women had proclaimed their independence when they bypassed the midi—were

Bonwit Teller, June 1954

poppycock. "Why then do they all wear the same fat furs, big boots, and blue jeans tattooed with the same designers' names? Bad taste is bad taste."

*D*uring his Bonwit years, perfume became a Moore specialty. Moore dislikes the smell of perfume but he loves working with it. "Perfume allows freedom for any fantasy," and he has sold it with images of seduction, abandonment, rapture, and betrayal. He has photographed women in trees and lagoons and taken pictures of Farley Granger tied to a chair, imprisoned by a scent. At Bonwit's he filled windows with large photographic blowups of eyes and over each pupil collaged the romantic vision each perfume promised, to relay with rigorous logic the breathtakingly simple message: Perfume affects the senses.

In his own favorite perfume display for Lenthéric in the old Savoy

Bonwit Teller, June 1954

Plaza Hotel, Moore gathered hydrangeas, pansies, and ferns, pressed them, then sandwiched the dried petals and fronds between sheets of plate glass. He placed a mirror at the window's back and the flowered glass at its front, transforming the space into a garden of dancing flowers and ferns. In another Lenthéric display, Moore filled windows with real flowering weeds dug from his garden and, by chance, a spider. "Those were fabulous, because the spider graciously spun a web."

*T*he reaction Moore likes almost as much as an "Ah!" is a smile. Humor is another Moore trademark, and all the people who know him comment on how his sense of humor informs his work. Gino DiGrandi once flew Moore to Rome to create an ad for Galliano featuring Gina Lollobrigida's favorite recipe, a version of Spaghetti Carbonara, using the liqueur. DiGrandi gave Moore a free hand, and after a day in Rome Moore said he needed a barn, a haystack,

Lollobrigida in an evening gown, and the sources of the recipe's ingredients: a pig for bacon, a chicken for eggs, and a goat for cheese. "We spent a day looking for everything," DiGrandi reports, "then Gina, who did not want to be photographed in a haystack or a barn, demurred. But she finally ended up in the haystack, dressed in satins, surrounded by the pig, the goat, and the chicken."

Moore's humor, which is gentle, suggestive, witty, and ironic, doesn't inspire big laughs. The book open to a picture of female genitalia gives the forbidden a goofy aspect. The ad for Spaghetti Carbonara depends on a take so obvious that the final image is as silly as it is witty. Moore's humor often grows out of wistful views. When he styled test shots of Linda Lovelace, star of the pornographic film *Deep Throat*, for

Vogue, July 1953. Photograph illustrating the perfume Sleeping by Schiaparelli

Vogue, July 1953. Photograph illustrating the perfume Cocktail Dry by Patou

Bonwit Teller, 1950s. Model, Cris Alexander. Perfume, My Sin by Lanvin

photographer Milton Greene, he dressed Lovelace in soft gowns and garlands so that she looked as innocent and ethereal as Botticelli's Venus. After the photographic session, Lovelace told Moore that no one had ever before paid so much attention to her.

Some jokes are private. A Bonwit window advertising Lanvin's perfume My Sin showed a startlingly beautiful model climbing out a window. On the desk in the room she is leaving lie her wedding ring and the farewell note "Beast." The window caused a commotion because no one in the trade had ever seen the model before. "Fashion editors and photographers wanted to know her name. I said she was Swedish and had gone home. What I couldn't tell them was that she was a he."

Moore's small office on the seventh floor of the Tiffany building is a jumble of objects: an abandoned jade plant he has nursed back to health, an antique doll a friend repaired, a carved Spanish horse from an old display, a photograph of Colette, and books on

Bonwit Teller, 1950s. Model, Cris Alexander. Perfume, Femme by Rochas

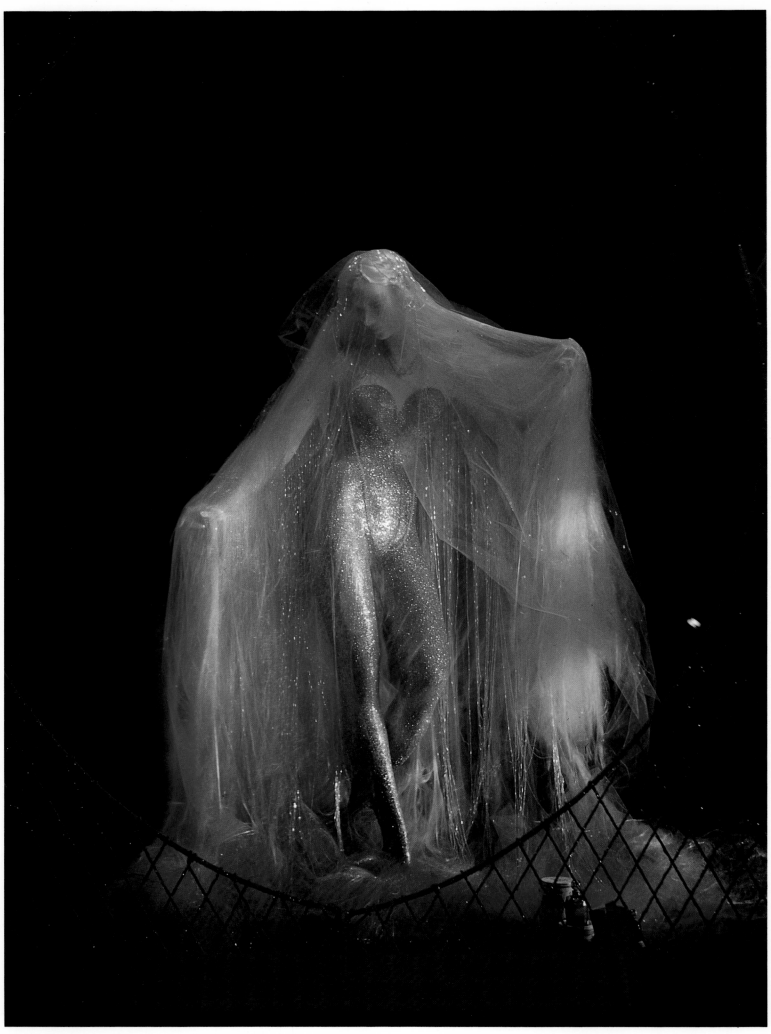

Bonwit Teller, December 12, 1948. Perfume, Calypso by Raucour

every conceivable subject: Greek coins, whales, Erté, wildflowers, birds of prey, Mother Goose, Henry Moore, Egyptian jewels, Shakespeare, the great houses of France, living reptiles of the world. Every surface holds reminders, souvenirs, plans for projects. The latticed-leather briefcase lying on the floor is a Moore design created for Gielgud's *Ides of March*. The desk is piled with papers, magazines, old telephone messages. The bag of jelly beans is a gift from a friend who knows of his addiction to dime-store candy. A telegram announcing Moore as the 1979 Display Man of the Year hangs from a bulletin board, along with a poster for a Robert Rauschenberg exhibition, a fading photograph of Norman Norell, a Manet reproduction, and a Gemini horoscope. In contrast to the room, Moore is a model of order. He wears impeccably tailored suits, favors shirts with French cuffs, and belongs to that special breed whose clothes do not wrinkle.

The small room is in a perpetually active state. Tiffany employees drop by unannounced. The phone rings continually. Artists call wanting jobs, and Moore's public, who assume he's as good-humored and high-spirited as his windows, call to pass along display suggestions or request information. Moore resents the time he spends talking to strangers; on busy days, he threatens to tear the phone from the wall, and if anyone is around when the phone rings, he expresses his irritation in elaborate pantomimes. "How am I supposed to work with this thing yapping at me?" Glaring at the ringing instrument, Moore barks at it, opening and closing his fingers in an up-and-down motion mimicking talk; his hand, like a fighter plane, swoops down toward the phone, attacking and buzzing it. Then, pleased by his charade, Moore answers the phone in a voice that still carries the soft sound of the South: "Yes, this is the real Gene Moore." He is accommodating to a fault, playful, and inordinately patient, particularly toward artists, explaining why he can't see their work or telling them when he can.

Since 1938, Moore has commissioned and shown work by over 800 artists. His own preferences do not influence what he puts in his windows. Moore likes Picasso, Vermeer, Joseph Cornell, dislikes most current abstraction (and most art dealers), seldom visits contemporary galleries, and was once quoted as saying that Pop art used too many display tricks. Moore will show any art, even an object he might not take home, if he thinks it will create a good display. "If people stop to look at the sculpture, they take in the jewels."

Moore's generosity toward artists has earned him the reputation of a patron of sorts. Young artists whom he has never met admire Moore's

work and follow his career. When told of his art world following, Moore ignores the compliment as if too worldly a reputation might get in his way. But when reminded that artists now famous remain grateful for his assignments or liked working with him, Moore beams with paternal pleasure. James Rosenquist mentions the Bonwit windows he made for Moore in every chronology of his career. Jasper Johns, who, with Robert Rauschenberg, designed windows under the joint nom de plume Matson Jones, remembers that Moore left them alone and that he always said, "Don't tell me, show me." Moore thought so highly of Matson Jones that he gave them special assignments. For a series of still lifes after seventeenth-century paintings he asked them to cast a pomegranate, a cantaloupe, a lemon, and a cabbage. "I want them to look as real as possible. I don't want them to look cast. I want them to have a painterly quality." Other assignments were less specific. For a series of landscapes he asked them to make a cave, a swamp, a seashore, a wishing well, a rock, and a highway.

*I*t was in June 1971 that Tiffany's windows featured the story of a jewel thief: the robber, a fragile gray papier-mâché mouse with an earnest and charming air, stole jewels from a safe; sold his booty to a fence; and, in top hat and tails, took his lady out to celebrate his money and his crime. In his final appearance, the mouse sits bereft, head in hands, slumped over, on a bare cot in jail.

Although the windows made the point that crime does not pay, on

June 9, 1971, Walter Hoving, then president of Tiffany's, received the following letter from Michael H. Thomas, then president of Cartier's: "Both from the point of view of one in the fine jewelry business and as a resident of midtown Manhattan, I must raise my voice in protest against your recent Fifth Avenue windows. I feel that raising attention to robberies and the hazards of owning fine jewelry are neither humorous nor appropriate." Hoving's reply, scrawled across the top of the letter, read: "Nuts, Walter Hoving."

Hoving's refined sense of the outrageous is a match for Moore's. In 1972, a garish Christmas tree display in front of First National City Bank's Park Avenue headquarters so upset Hoving that he ran an advertisement in the *Wall Street Journal* (it had been rejected by the *New York Times*) which read: "Dear First National City Bank, We are very sad to see that you are once again polluting the esthetic atmosphere of Park Avenue by lighting the loud and vulgar Christmas tree on Park Avenue and 53rd Street.... So we earnestly urge you to put out those glaring lights. If you do, you will be practicing good esthetics on a par with the good banking for which you are justifiably famous."

Moore has worked for Hoving for thirty-five years—sixteen years at Bonwit Teller, when Hoving was its president, and twenty-five at Tiffany's (for six years he worked for both stores simultaneously)—and when Moore talks about working for Tiffany's, he means working for Hoving. He thinks Hoving has more foresight than any merchant he has ever known. "He's always willing to try something new, and if it doesn't work, he doesn't mind having taken the chance. He will listen to anyone with taste." Like Moore, Hoving believes in good taste, good design, and old-fashioned durability. Tiffany's sells more than the accouterments of the good life. There is an aspect of their merchandising that goes beyond the security conferred by owning Waterford crystal or Royal Crown Derby china; it is a moral attitude, grounded in Calvinist homilies. Tiffany's customers know that they get what they pay for; they also know that the best things in life can be very expensive.

Moore regards Hoving as his aesthetic protector. When Hoving hired Moore he said, "You have carte blanche. Do what you want. But don't try to sell anything." To others he said, "Don't ask Gene what he's going to do. He'll show you." Hoving has "left Moore alone." In twenty-five years he has taken exception to only one window; when he commented that a sculpture with kinetic fingers suggested an off-color gesture, Moore replied, "Mr. Hoving, some people have dirty minds."

Hoving makes only one demand. Every year at Easter Moore must install a live Easter lily, with a Bible open to the Gospels.

*F*inding jewels in Tiffany's windows has become something of a New York sport, like searching for Ninas in an Al Hirschfeld drawing. Looking like afterthoughts, diamonds glisten in sand, sparkle in seashells, decorate gumdrop-filled ice-cream cones. The worm that a bird tugs from the earth is a dazzling bracelet. A toy crane lifts a necklace from a pile of dirt. An elaborate brooch sits on a golf tee. A necklace twists around a submerged anchor. But sometimes whole designs are built with merchandise. Moore has stacked crystal wineglasses, one precariously on top of another, and has used water-filled cut-crystal goblets to rinse paintbrushes. He has drawn pictures with sterling, played ticktacktoe using bone china plates as O's and crisscrossing knives and forks as X's, written messages on stationery, and plucked porcelain animals from the obscurity of the china department for two weeks in the limelight.

Moore chooses merchandise at the very last minute. On the day before installations, he roams the store until something catches his fancy. He seldom knows in advance what he'll find. The buyers do not pressure him, and management never tells him what to display. Everyone knows that Moore has distinct preferences and cannot be influenced. He likes garnets, opals, coral, jade, aquamarines. He doesn't like diamonds, except as accessories to highlight other stones. He prefers rubies to sapphires and likes flawed rubies best. He likes emeralds even better because he's never seen one without a flaw—which he thinks is "very considerate of them." Given his choice, Moore says, he would gaze at an opal.

What ends up in a window has little to do with Moore's taste for the understated, the semiprecious, and the flawed. His sole criterion is what looks best. But Moore's casual attitude toward merchandise belies his serious regard for display. A window must engage the viewer after it stops him. A window is an invitation into the store. To Moore, windows are like the clothes one wears. "They announce who you are and what you think of yourself. Even if no one's well-groomed anymore, my windows are."

Moore keeps a running tally on how windows sell. At times this has come in handy. Some years ago, at Bonwit's, when Moore asked for a raise, he was told that he could have his raise if he cut his display budget by one percent. The suggestion was ludicrous (the display field is notoriously underbudgeted), and as an alternative Moore proposed that his raise equal one percent of all sales made from windows. Management, thinking Moore did not have access to the information, agreed, until Moore presented them with receipts and a sales total. "They didn't give me one percent of sales, but they didn't cut my budget, and I got my raise."

Although the merchandise in Moore's windows appears as dashed off as a postscript, it plays a calculated role in the visual drama. Cast to reveal daft puns and surprising dénouements, merchandise often holds the secret to the plot, invariably making the point that merchandise, after all, is the point. In windows featuring model cars, Moore showed a toy dump truck filled with dirt and a diamond. The gesture of setting a diamond in dirt is stylishly cavalier, and it sold diamonds. Presenting diamonds as a natural element, plentiful enough to be disposable, made the large rock accessible. It also solved the riddle posed to passing window shoppers, who, once they saw the diamond, realized they were not gazing into the windows of F.A.O. Schwarz or a construction company, but into those of New York's famous jewelry store, wherein resides the privilege required to throw diamonds in dirt.

On Valentine's Day, Tiffany's windows feature sentiments of chronic romantics, and merchandise plays the leading role as the gift of love.

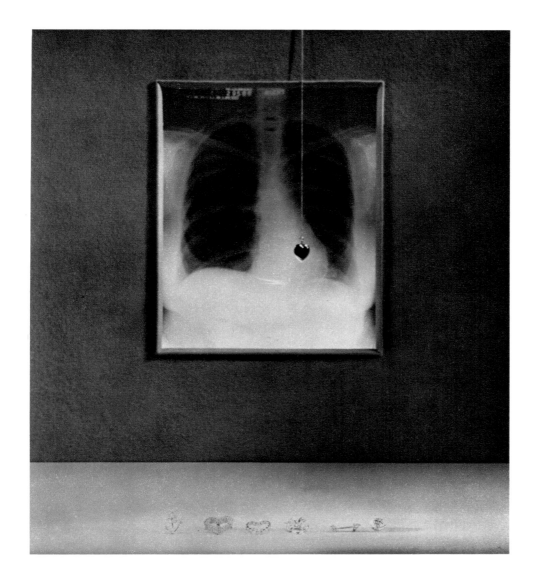

There's no shilly-shallying; corny windows peddle love's trinkets. Moore gives gold diggers and young lovers equal time, every year finding new ways to say "Diamonds are forever" and "Diamonds are a girl's best friend." He has hung a gold heart in the exact anatomical position over a film of a chest X-ray; shown a floating hand with a stethoscope listening to the rhythm of another gold heart; and placed a heart blazing with jewels next to a handwritten recipe for Julia Child's Coeurs Flambés. When he built the words "Love you" with white gumdrops on a fuchsia ground, they were reminiscent of a theater marquee, flashing a love letter from Tiffany's to its clients. When he constructed the word "Love" from cubes of sugar, he studded the sugar with diamond pins and feeding birds, conjuring up every phrase from Sweetie Pie to Sugar Daddy; the nibbling birds further complicated the message by hinting that love was nourishing and also for the birds.

Many displays reveal Moore's nascent cynicism. One Valentine's Day, he laid a shattered piece of plate glass on top of a painted red heart. The bow that had dealt the blow hung in the air above; an arrow rose from the heart's center, and a diamond-and-ruby bracelet circled around it. The elaborate pantomime of heartbreak included a wry reassurance, a glittering panacea: Jewels mend broken hearts.

Sometimes, as in the miniature rooms Moore showed in October 1978, merchandise appears completely incidental. Designed by New

November 1, 1978. Miniature room, one of the series of five built by Edward Acevedo. Design by Parish-Hadley, Inc.

York decorators Mario Buatta, Angelo Donghia, Vladimir Kagan, Kevin McNamara, and Parish-Hadley, and built by Edward Acevedo, the rooms ranged from a space that Southern Californians might inhabit, filled with modernistic furniture, a minuscule replica of a Frank Stella painting, and a sunken fireplace pit to a sunny, pale-yellow living room with copies of Impressionist pictures and furniture covered in floral-patterned fabrics. Scaled one inch to one foot, the rooms held dogs, cats, tiny vases filled with bite-size flowers, and large jewels—brooches and earrings—in unlikely places.

Tiffany's advertised the rooms in the *New York Times,* and for their opening hosted a breakfast reception on Fifth Avenue. The invitation to the vernissage read: "You are cordially invited to breakfast in front of Tiffany's." The entire week before the event, Moore appeared preoccupied. Although the invitation's wording was literally correct, Moore would have preferred "breakfast at Tiffany's," and he thought Truman Capote and Audrey Hepburn should have been invited. Moore wanted the event to be splendid; accustomed to running the show, he was uncomfortable not handling every detail. The reception began promptly at ten o'clock on a mild, blue-skied day. The corner of Fifty-seventh and Fifth was crowded, and only a thin white ribbon separated shoppers and workers from the breakfast guests. A personable lady stood behind the ribbon, checking off guests' names as she welcomed them with the So-nice-to-see-you's one expects to hear at a private party. No uninvited guests attempted to join the reception, and it occurred to a number of those present that Tiffany's might be the only New York institution that still had the authority to keep order at a busy corner during the morning rush hour.

The crowd included reporters, decorators, buyers, Henry Platt, Tiffany's president, who is also a great-grandson of Louis Comfort Tiffany, and Walter Hoving, Tiffany's chairman and chief executive officer. In black overcoat and black homburg, smiling broadly, Mr. Hoving towered over everyone else, looking like a benevolent despot. Moore stood separate from the crowd, watching it. At one point he said: "I hate parties; these are Edward's windows, not mine, and even if they were mine,

Design by Angelo Donghia

Design by Vladimir Kagan

I'd want to go upstairs." But then he caught sight of a friend, and his sad eyes took on a neon glint and he started moving in and out of the crowd with the ease of a professional party-goer. The presence of old friends pleased him, and he was cheered when Mr. Hoving complimented the windows.

"He is a remarkable man," Moore said, nodding his head in Hoving's direction.

"He looks like a patriarch," said the woman next to him.

"Yes," Moore replied. "That can be a blessing and a problem."

At eleven o'clock sharp, as promptly as it began, the reception ended. By then the windows were drawing crowds three and four people deep; they captured the public's fancy because miniature rooms represent the best of all possible worlds. They are small utopias, whose inhabitants do not suffer colds or worry about the rent. In miniature, anyone can live in a room designed by an expensive and exclusive New York decorator.

The rooms were as effective as they were popular, and Tiffany's, for the first time in its history, held the windows over and placed ads in the daily papers announcing the extended run. The very first day a pair of Angela Cummings earrings sold off the couch in the Southern California living room, and Moore was off roaming the store to find a replacement. He complained because he couldn't find anything he liked as much, but he was pleased by the windows' success: "You know the jewels were the trick. Their scale threw everything out of kilter. They made the rooms into the fantasies they really were, and gave the jewels an urgent reality."

Throughout the miniature rooms' three-week run, the doll windows that had preceded them hung in Moore's mind. One afternoon, during a lunch at Larre's, Moore was in the middle of a sentence, describing the Philharmonic concert he'd attended the night before, when he interrupted himself to say he would do the dolls again some day, and that he'd just commissioned a new set of miniature rooms. "The same," he said, smiling, "but different."

The doll windows didn't appear the next year. But on a stony gray

November morning, Tiffany's hosted another breakfast reception. Scaffolding had unexpectedly appeared overnight along the store's Fifty-seventh Street side, but Moore remained impervious to the disruption as he stood by, a quiet impresario, watching the crowd that had come to see New York's best street theater. Once again people were standing three and four deep in front of the smallest shopwindows in the world for a glimpse of the stuff of dreams: a rustic room in a Swiss chalet, a formal parlor with a pint-size grand piano, a duplex penthouse with a floating staircase and a view of New York harbor, a pale-blue bedroom for a star, and a tranquil living room with the air of the East—fantasy rooms designed by New York decorators for Audrey Hepburn, Zubin Mehta, Mikhail Baryshnikov, Dorothy Loudon, and Bill Blass.

Moore's windows reflect a steady progress. They have grown gradually sparer and more abstract. Narratives have been compressed. But themes remain the same, complicated and universal. Repetition doesn't worry Moore. He is forever revising himself, taking the same themes and materials and reusing them differently. Every window leads to another, although a decade may pass before it appears. The windows at Tiffany's are Moore's own; he does not depend on merchandise. He can create whatever sideshow he likes out of whatever materials he chooses. Still, he listens to the pulse of his audience: he always replays a crowd pleaser like the miniature rooms. But if given a choice, Moore returns to nature.

"I keep trying," Moore says, "to get down to basics, to the real feeling. Over the years I've gotten simpler. I use less merchandise. In the beginning I'd use five rings, now I'll only use one. But there are certain things I can't stop using—birds, seashells, butterflies, and eggs. They constantly pass through my life, and somehow I always find a place for them. Sometimes I worry. Easter is coming up, and I'll think, how many things can I do with eggs? I've done twenty-five years of eggs. I've shown one egg and eight hundred eggs and broken eggs. I know I've laid a lot of eggs. But eggs are so beautiful, more beautiful than a sphere. No two eggs are alike, and every egg symbolizes a beginning."

TASTE IN THE

MARKETPLACE

by Gene Moore

*F*irst, the displayman must make his audience stop and look. This is just as true for the artist, sculptor, composer, or any other creator. The displayman is a creator.

When someone looks into a Tiffany window, I want him to do a double —even a triple—take. I want him to experience the sudden fresh insight that the Zen philosophers call the "ahness" of things. It is also called the thrill of discovery. It happens when you suddenly see something as if for the first time. Humor and surprise are elements that help create the effect.

Another element that contributes to a double take is contrast. Contrast is a most important element in good display design. The item being displayed is framed or highlighted by the contrasting element, and this again makes it possible—if you choose your contrasting materials with originality and wit— to startle the viewer into looking, and looking again.

Economy of materials is another important element in good display design. The fewer distractions, the stronger the effect. Contrast is emphasized by economy. The resulting astringency helps focus the eye and the attention.

The displayman, especially the window displayman, can never forget that his primary function is to sell an item of merchandise or the image of the store. To sell, you must make people see with a fresh eye—as if they'd never seen a purse or a pair of shoes before. Further, you want to involve them with the very essence of purse or shoe or leather.

No ambition is too high-flown for the displayman. The differences between him and the sculptor, painter, and composer have more to do with the materials he works with than with standards of taste and ambition. Quality is what you do with what you have. There is no reason that a displayman can't have quality with tissue paper and twine as well as canvas and bronze. Anything can increase our awareness of the world around us if we have the eyes to see. If the displayman believes this, and has this as a goal, he'll sell. We displaymen must catch the eye of the passerby if we are to sell, but we must not catch it with an inappropriate bang or any other offensive and irrelevant means—or we will be selling bad taste. Everything we displaymen do is selling. If we want to sell diamonds, then we must sell the environment of diamonds, the meaning of diamonds, the excitement of diamonds, as well as the gems themselves.

A good example of the use of contrast and economy is showing Tiffany diamonds in the windows on piles of sand. The sand is in one sense the antithesis of diamonds. It makes a good frame for diamonds. The contrast makes diamonds look even more diamondy than ever: they sparkle in the gritty, dull sand; they are one among a trillion sand specks. It is amusing to think of such a precious thing as a diamond tossed onto sand. It reminds you, humorously, how very precious diamonds are.

But you must use your props in fresh, unsuspected ways. I like very elegant or very earthy ones—like burlap, pasta, wire, bark, sheet music, moss, rubber bands, road maps, rocks, hay, tin cans, the insides of clocks. If this sounds like James Thurber, it is with good reason. Thurber would have made a great displayman—he was forever making you see things afresh and with humor. He combined the possible with the impossible so blithely that the impossible became right, and what you expected seemed absurd. Thurber also had the genius to make you feel that he was writing or talking just to you, to you alone. This is another quality the displayman tries to get into display—that warm, intimate, personal involvement with human beings.

The problem is that window areas are too limited. I don't mean just in size. There are other limitations that stifle. But we must use everything at hand—light, sound, water, the double and triple take, three dimensionality, everything—every way you can find to abrade the awareness of the audience, to make the looker start and say "Ah!"

Window display, in fact all display design, has much in common with decorating and architecture and the arts. Perhaps the most important of these common qualities—I think it is the most important consideration in architecture and decorating and design today—is human scale. The human touch. Humanity. Buildings, rooms, display, all involve people. Design in these areas must be human, too. Architects forget all too often that people are going to walk and live in their buildings and rooms. Buildings that

look splendid on paper may look dreadful when they have people in them. People must look well in the buildings, in the rooms, and in connection with display. One good example of this human involvement is New York's Philharmonic hall. Seen from the street, the promenades that surround the outside of the building on three sides look marvelous with people moving about in them. And people *feel* marvelous moving about on the promenades. If you are going to sell merchandise or image, you must involve warmth and people.

Scale is one way. Humor is the most difficult and the most successful way. Every time people smile at one of my windows, I know they "get" it, and are involved with it. Somehow they've made it their own. Thirty years ago, store managers thought that the way to sell was to fill the windows with more and more merchandise. They thought that the more they showed, the more would be bought. But it didn't work. Then the bold ones tried showing just one or two items, and items in recognizable situations. That worked.

True, Dali and Surrealism had a lot to do with the growth of window display design, and Dali isn't humanistic in the sense I have in mind. But Dali took commonplace, everyday things—like watches and people and pianos—and did such strange things to them that anyone who looked would see things freshly, see to the inner essence. The dripping watch, the drawers that pull out of human bodies, the holes in stomachs and heads—all these devices are startling ways to make you look and think about watch works and human works. Dali is a great displayman. The trouble is that catching the eye is important but it must be done with taste, with humor, with human warmth, and with imagination. That is hard to do.

Sad to say, but not surprisingly, display design is in a rut. The spurt of growth is over. There are many serious and crippling limitations to window display. All the possible solutions to these problems have been explored over and over again. A great limitation to window display growth is physical—the windows themselves.

1. The shape of the windows is set; they are all boxes of one permanent size. This is not only unnecessary but a terrible handicap. Windows should have shutters like a camera, to make it possible to focus on a purse or back up to show a room or a scene.

2. Everything that can be done in a rectangle—and that is what a window is—has been done. We need to be able to change not only

the size but the shape of windows, and easily. A window should be able to become round or deep or narrow or triangular. There should be floors that drop away, backs that move away, catwalks for the lighting engineers, sides that move away.

3. Windows should be so flexible, in short, that rooms can be created in them. That is not possible today; there is no depth. A room should not just be suggested. If it's to be a room display, a window should *be* a room.

4. Windows should be air-conditioned so that fresh flowers, for example, can be used with lasting power. Windows should be heated in winter. They should be air-tight and sealed off from the rest of the store so that no extraneous and unwanted breezes distract, so that air jets can be installed for directed breezes. There should be water sources, so that there can be waterfalls, pools, streams. There should be fireproofing so that flame can be used. There should be room for lights, good lights. Lighting is at least fifty percent of display. You can make or break a display with light. Yet, in spite of this, windows are so narrow that lights cannot be angled but must flood directly. Light should make shadows, enhance texture, create atmosphere.

In short, all the elements—earth, air, fire, and water—should be in the tool kit of the displayman.

I am talking of the limits of store and window architecture. I will go further. Window display should include the whole first floor of the store. Let the literal selling—the exchange of money for items—go on on the second floor. Give us displaymen the ground floor for displaying the merchandise, using all the materials of nature and the contrivances of man to create with. This is our rightful stage. I am in fact describing a technically lavish theater—a miniature Radio City Music Hall, or better.

Another kind of limit to the growth of window display is budget. A full-page ad in the *New York Times* costs thousands of dollars. It runs a day. It is seen by hundreds of thousands of people. Whoever heard of a window displayman having a comparable budget for his windows (except in a rare instance at Christmas time)? Yet during a week of the life of a window display on Fifth Avenue more than a million people walk by and are exposed to the windows.

Display should not expect to have the same budget and status as general advertising, because it is more limited than mass media advertising in many ways. Of course, it is freer in some ways, too. But display deserves far more status and a larger budget than it has. The status of the window as a selling tool needs to go up—and drastically and fast. And the status of the displayman needs to go up, too. The change in windows, since quantity of items displayed has been removed as *the* criterion, has created a whole new audience—in fact a whole new national pastime, called window shopping, night-time strolling on the Avenue, or Sunday shopping.

Without a reduction of the limitations I have described, window display will lose its appeal; there will be nothing new to catch the eye, nothing tasteful. This is beginning to happen. For the last five years the development has slowed. Soon people will get bored. They will stop looking in windows. Already the eye-catching quality is becoming less and less in good taste. I have seen, for example, mannequins looking like call girls. They may be eye stoppers, but they are contradicting the quality of the store image and the merchandise that is being sold.

The answer lies in the displaymen themselves and in the fields of serious art. Display takes its lead from art trends. As long as there is sterility in the arts—and I believe there is—there will be sterility in display and, I believe, also in decorating. Architecture leads interior decoration as well as display. Architecture is stumbling, too. Decorators are constantly looking for new ways. But newness for its own sake isn't enough and we all know that.

Unless the limitations are lessened and removed and unless the leading creators develop new rich areas involving human warmth and sound ideas, display will continue to get boring, fewer and fewer people will look, and the impact of window display will decline. I am very pessimistic. There is nothing new, nothing daring. I see bad taste being used as an eye catcher. I see more and more fear on the part of the purse-string holders. Four people in conference can kill any idea, no matter how good it is. I am waiting for an imaginative architect and a courageous store management to meet and build me the windows I want and have described. I am waiting full of hope and very eagerly. But I am waiting.

Remarks delivered at a symposium held at Town Hall, New York, in 1962.

VALENTINES

"An old Valentine engraving...I cut it up like a jigsaw puzzle, took the cut-out pieces and laid them on the floor, and then just lined up the hearts."

"The knitted heart was done in very heavy red yarn. I called a friend and said, 'I want a red heart and I want it this size, and leave the knitting needles in at the top.' Very simple."

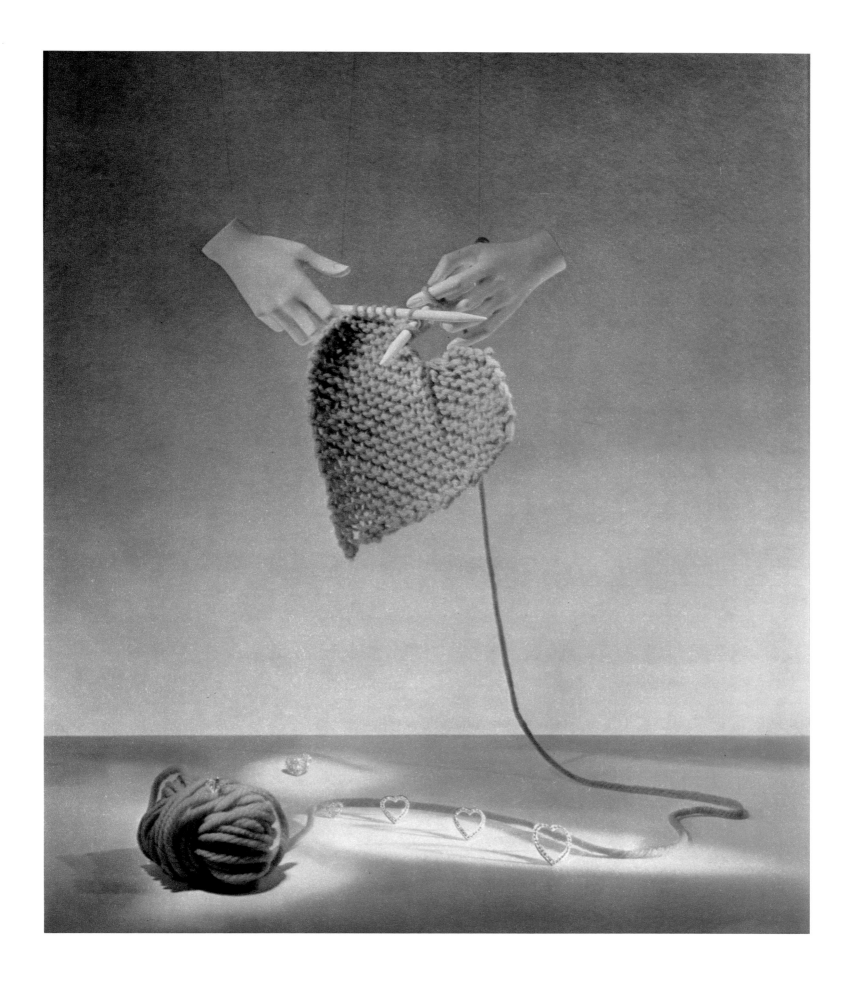

"When I didn't do letters one Valentine's Day, they were missed. People love reading other people's mail. Letters are successful every time. Even if I place them upside down, people stand there and read them.

"For Whistler's Valentine to his mother, I put her flowers in a lovely old silver teapot. Whistler was very fond of his mother, and I think she was the only person who ever called him Jamie. So I wrote, 'My own darling Mother, Your portrait is an enormous success. Will you be my Valentine? Your loving son, Jamie.' And I put a butterfly in the window—his usual signature on his paintings."

"For Julia Child, the great chef lady, a bouquet of fresh vegetables. Both bouquets had to be changed every day. But you don't feel put upon—you feel happy to do something that people like and that has meaning for them. I feel very connected to my public. It's like being an actor. If I lose them, I'm lost."

"This old cash register turned out to be great as a Valentine theme. On all those keys I put names. . . . You push whomever you want and the total appears above in hugs and kisses instead of dollars and cents. Then the money drawer opens up and offers you gumdrops and candy hearts instead of cold cash!"

"Love, love, love, love. Gumdrops and rhinoceroses. Red gumdrops up against the face of the window, and rhinos from the China Department touching noses. And love in various languages—in Swahili, in Spanish, in English—this time in sugar cubes, with love birds playing around."

"This is one of my favorite sets of Valentine windows—enormous blow-ups of movie stills. They were four by four feet, and they really captured the eye. I got the stills at the Museum of Modern Art's wonderful Film Stills Archive. And, using five different handwritings, I wrote a Valentine billet-doux for each couple. I tried to imagine what Wallace Beery might have said to Marie Dressler; W.C. Fields to his little chickadee, Mae West; Greta Garbo to John Gilbert; Judy Garland to Mickey Rooney; William Powell to Myrna Loy—in their film roles, of course!"

"Feb. 14
Ahoy Min,
You tug at
my heart.
 Ha Ha,
 Bill"

"February 14th
Flower Belle, my Angel:
Be my little Chickadee.
Be mine to woo—
Your devoted servant,
Cuthbert J. Twilly"

"February 14th
Dearest Leo:
I want to be alone—
with you, my darling!
Ever,
Felicitas"

"February 14th
Golly gee, Andy—
    You're swell and
so very generous.
Love,
        Betsy"

"February 14th
Dear Nora:
        Have a heart—
Have a martini—
        See you later.
Love,
        Nick"

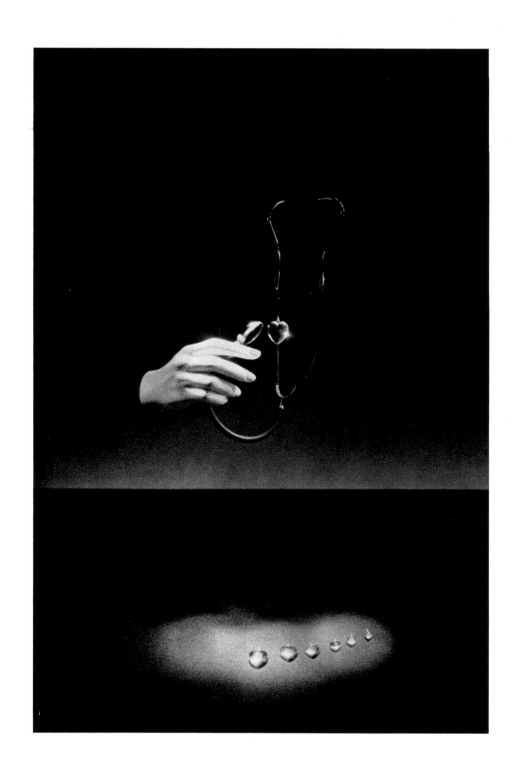

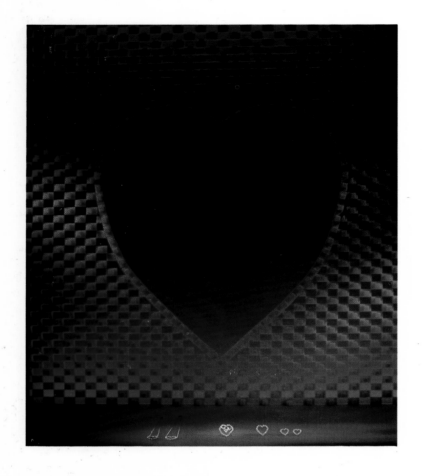

"Working with sugar cubes is tricky. You have to get the glue all over the sticking side, but not too much, or the cube will melt before you get it attached. The whole thing was done on a piece of plate glass, so you really looked right through it."

"The wooden heart was one I had carved a long time ago, and I've used it in many ways. Knocking those crazy holes in it was a Magritte touch."

"The old scale, anyone can see, is very accurate. Those are stones in the right-hand pan, but a heart outweighs stones, that's clear."

IMAGE
AND
SPECTACLE

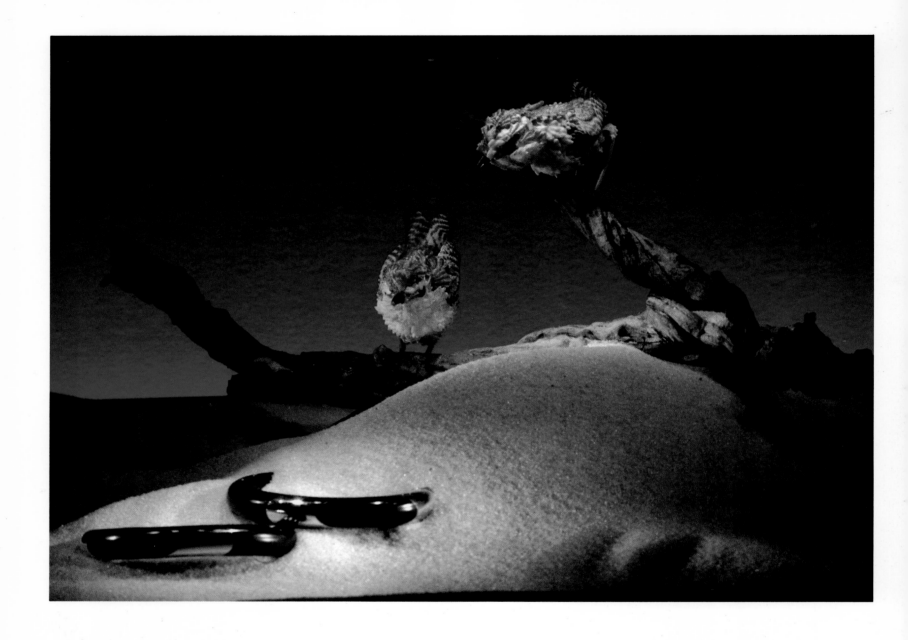

"In these two seashore windows, the materials the artists used are as different as they could possibly be, and the results are both fantastic. The birds were made of seashells. Imagine finding exactly the right shells—as Ruth Ross did—to follow a bird's shape with. And the construction, by Edmund Neimann, is made of wooden tongue depressors. Construction isn't really the right word—it's so beautiful it should be called sculpture."

"These are sand sculptures, at least they're all covered with sand. They have a sort of Eastern look. The buildings' roofs were made with jello molds; the walls were boxes. Ronald Prybycien was the builder.

"The square cave is plaster covered in sand, and there's sand on the floor. Again, the feeling is Eastern. That's why I used the serpentine brace-let. Considering that I have only twenty-two inches, the windows look very deep. I could have lit the back, but that would have made the window look shallow. Keeping the back dark and the front light creates depth and adds a certain mystery."

"In tribute to the Philharmonic, the strings in this window are real harp strings. Of course they're not graded in length the way they would be in the instrument, but they're not arranged helter-skelter. First I got the strings and then I found out, from someone who knew how a harp is strung, which string went next to which string. Then I got in the window and I stapled each string, top and bottom. It took hours, but it was worth all the trouble because it came out right. The strings were up against the glass and the candelabrum was behind the strings."

"Again, this was for the beginning of a new Philharmonic season. Here I wanted to show the power of sound. How better to do this than by having real hands come out of a real kettledrum and break a real glass?"

"The occasion for the ballet window was the wonderful new book on the New York City Ballet that came out in 1973. The dancer is one of those little articulated artists' figures. A strange thing about them is that you can make them look male or female by the position you put them into."

"In April and May of 1962 there was a big Picasso event in New York. Nine leading galleries simultaneously exhibited his works, and the project was called Picasso: An American Tribute. *The chairman asked me—and the display people of several other stores—to do Picasso windows. On the night of the opening of the exhibition there was a special bus to take people around to all the various windows.*

"*What I did was to select some paintings and have them reproduced three-dimensionally by cutting out the elements. The table, the feet, the heads, all protrude. Ron McNamer executed this project. Everything was painted from scratch exactly like the original. The only difference was the dimensionality, which, quite frankly, I thought enhanced the paintings!*"

"In the windows with reproductions of Greek heads (I bought them in a shop that sells plaster casts) I wanted to show what each one of the people was thinking about. So I took a saw and I sawed a piece out of each head. Then I had to fill it in with plaster to create a surface there, since the casts were hollow of course. I painted the heads black, which was effective because you're not accustomed to seeing these things black, and I put the sawed-out pieces of the heads on the floor. Clearly, this person has time on his mind."

"For a series of windows on Greece, I borrowed the bronze sculpture from Robsjohn-Gibbings' collection. It's of a Greek actor's foot wearing the platform sole of the ancient Greek tragedian. I just hung a drapery in the back. It's a piece of linen that I dipped in tea to make it look old. It adds scale tremendously because of the shadows—they make the difference. The jewelry—the pins—reminded me very much of the fastenings that were worn on Greek mantles to hold them together up on the shoulder."

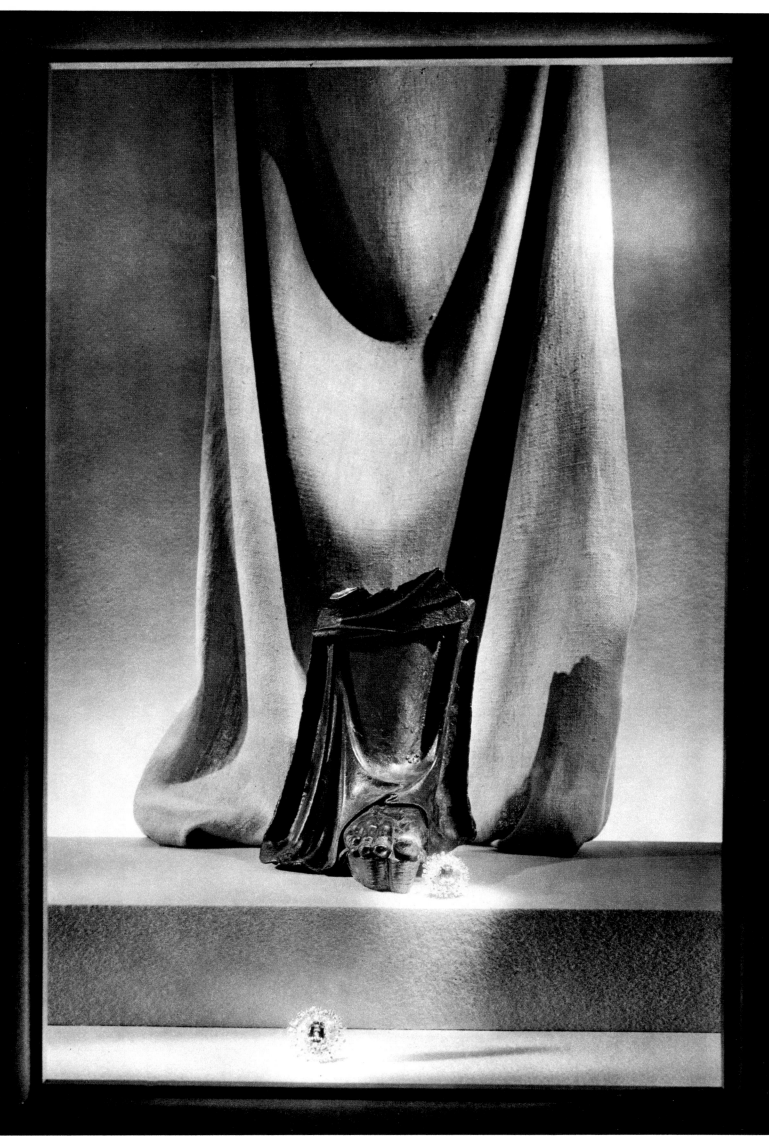

"These windows are based on Palladio, the great six-teenth-century Italian architect. I found two old books of engravings of his work, and I blew the engravings up pho-tographically. For the arches I made two enlargements, mounted them on board, cut them all out, and put one in front of the other to create a third dimension. To go with them, I needed a number of objects that would be similar and architectural; that's why I used the glasses there."

"One page in the Palladio books showed different types of columns—capitals, really—and I decided I wanted real Corinthian, Doric, and Ionic capitals. So I made them out of wood, and then I could put merchandise on them. I haunted junk shops to find those little figures, because there was almost always statuary on top of Palladio's buildings. The figures were in the engravings, but I wanted real fig-ures, for dimension."

"I wanted to show a pitcher pouring water, so I got the pitcher, I got the glass, and I said to the artist, Jordan Steckel, 'Look, I want water pouring from the pitcher.' I gave him the length that I wanted, and he did it. He glued together very thin strips of balsa wood, thinner than matchsticks. Very fragile. Transporting these creations was almost as much of a feat as making them.

"In hanging one marvelous geometric shape, I dropped it. So I just let it lie there. It broke so elegantly that I thought, 'Why should I even bother to do anything? I can't mend it. Just leave it. It's beautiful.'"

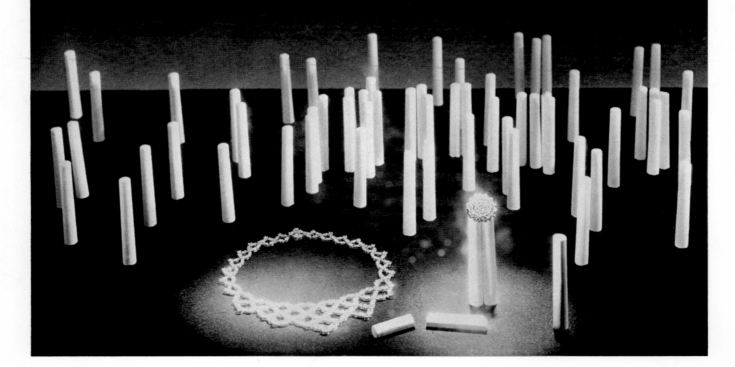

"The chalk window was one of a series on drawing and painting media—oil paint, watercolor, and so on. Chalk is almost everyone's first medium, and as a kid almost everyone has gone up to the blackboard and drawn figures like this one. I know I did. So I drew the figure and made all those pieces of chalk stand up. Wasn't easy. I had to glue each piece onto the felt covering the floor. I use felt a lot because it has a nice texture to it and comes six feet wide."

"Windows come about in odd ways. An artist friend, Robin Thew, told me of a dream her little girl had had. It seems the child was mad for horses, and envious of other children who were lucky enough to have horses of their own. All she had was a bicycle. In her sleep she dreamed about horses— about having an ice-cream soda with a horse, about flying on Pegasus, and finally about turning into a horse. I said to the mother, 'It would be fabulous to have that dream in the windows. I want you to do it for me.' So she did!"

"The little articulated artists' figures are among my favorite props. You can do so much with them. They come absolutely plain, in natural wood. You can put them in almost any position, and you can really feel the tension in those bodies.

"I guess I always wanted to be an acrobat when I was a kid, and I love harlequins and the commedia dell'arte. So I painted some figures and made them harlequin hats. Each one of the men in the acrobatic setup was holding a ring. The impossible balance of their act was managed by gluing them together. I love impossible things; they always make people smile."

*"Baseball, golf, badminton, fishing, bowling...I know how many peo-
ple I see reading the sports pages all the time on the bus, so I thought they—
especially men—would like these windows. You don't always stop the men!
This was in the Spring, and I painted sky backgrounds that were quite
pretty. I bought all the stuff at a sporting goods store but I painted everything black, except the bowling pins, which I painted white. It made more
sense that way, wasn't so commercial-looking. And it provided a surreal foil
for the bracelets and rings."*

"The butterfly is one of Dove Bradshaw's beautiful stained-glass works. It's suspended, and the lighting makes it cast wonderful shadows. In front of the whole thing I put netting to soften it up, to create a kind of haze. Besides, nets go with butterflies. One thinks of butterfly nets, butterflies flying against nets, butterflies flying against screens."

"Luckily, when I got the idea of doing a shoe in peacock feathers, I knew just the person to turn to. So I took the peacock feathers to Beth Levine and selected the shoe I wanted, and she made a pair. She loved the idea so much that she kept the other one!"

124

"William Harnett is one of my favorite painters, and I was thinking of him when I was trying to get these compositions together, wondering how, if he had been a window trimmer, he would have done it. I had fun mixing merchandise with the found objects I was using—the wooden dipper, the

horseshoe, those old pistols. They were all mounted on real wood planks
that I stained and rubbed down to dull them. To get the look of those great
shadows in Harnett's paintings, after I'd done the lighting I intensified the
shadows it created, crouching in that little space with my paintbox."

"Euclid got me permanently interested in geometric shapes. These were part of a series of geometric windows. There was nothing that could possibly be shown with a white sphere except pearls, so far as I was concerned. So I got the string of pearls—they were real Oriental ones, not cultured—and when I got into the window I decided the only thing to do was to break the string. 'That's the only way it would work,' I said in answer to complaints. Then, another decision made in the window: I suspended the end of the pearls in the air a bit, which helped the composition of the whole thing and gave it more life."

"The Escher-like construction I comissioned from a woodworker. Floating in midair it worked quite well. If it had been a solid box, it would have been very dull as a shape, unlike a sphere, which is not dull, ever."

"There was no other way I could do this construction except right in the window. Particularly because I didn't know what I was going to do. I did know I was going to hang crystal, and I wanted the glasses to be as fragile as possible. I wonder now how it came out looking so well from the front, when I was working backwards. I guess I must see the way you see in a camera, which is upside down. I remember that I took black paint and painted out the cord in places—it was against a black background—so that the line just seemed to stop in space. If it had gone all the way through, it wouldn't have been nearly as good. That's the interesting thing about it."

"But cat's cradle is another story. It's one thing that has always fascinated me but I could never do. Too complicated. I had to get someone who knew how to do it to really give me lessons, for this window. And now I've forgotten it again!"

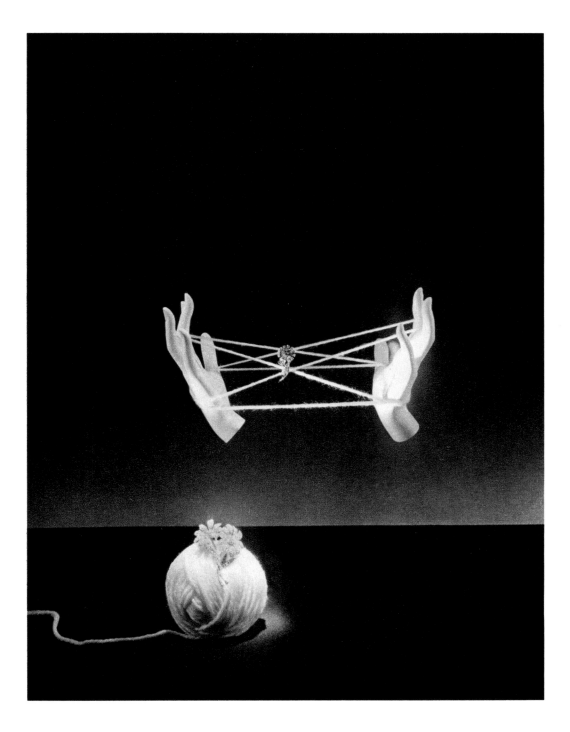

"*The twine windows might never have happened if I hadn't found a few balls of the stuff upstairs. I thought, 'The color is so great! How marvelous it would be against burlap.'*

"*So this set of windows didn't cost a nickel. It's the kind of thing I love doing because it's crazy—and simple. I wound the big ball of twine myself, out of the cord we use to wrap with in the store. And the jewel trails off as if it were a piece of nothing.*"

"I ran across a book called Knots, *and was impressed by all the things that could be done with rope. So we spent a lot of time making real, true knots the way they would be made by an honest-to-God knot-maker—or sailor. Some of the knots looked like designs; they were very complicated. But my favorite rope window is the piece of rope with one simple knot tied in it, on which a butterfly in pink tourmaline, diamonds, and gold has alighted."*

"How did I drive the nail through the glass without shattering it? How does a magician saw a woman in half? It's a trick! I had a glazier drill me two holes in the glass and I shoved a nail through them. You couldn't see that the holes were drilled at all because the nail fitted into them exactly."

"In this one of a series of windows with glasses, the glasses were being used for washing out the paintbrushes. So there's different-colored water in each one."

"Suspension, and suspense too! All those glasses balanced on a board, which is balanced on a sawhorse. Someone is sawing through the board, so you know the glasses are all going to fall and break. Everything was painted white—the sawhorse, the board, the saw, and the background. Nothing to distract from the tension of waiting for the glasses to fall."

"The ancient water pump and the old ax I found out in the country. I'd been saving them for years. I save everything I find because I know some day it will come in handy. I keep all this stuff in my office—it's quite a junk shop. Duco cement on a piece of cloth made the icy water pouring out of the pump."

"Here Jasper Johns and Robert Rauschenberg turned their hands to outdoor scenes. They could do anything and make anything. I never knew who did what; they worked together on everything. The enormous stone—we could never have lifted a stone that heavy into the windows—was all made of papier-mâché and then painted. The ground was covered in real dirt, and the poles in the ravine were standing in real water. A circulating pump kept the water moving slightly. I painted all the sky backgrounds myself—somber, lowering skies to go with the desolate landscapes."

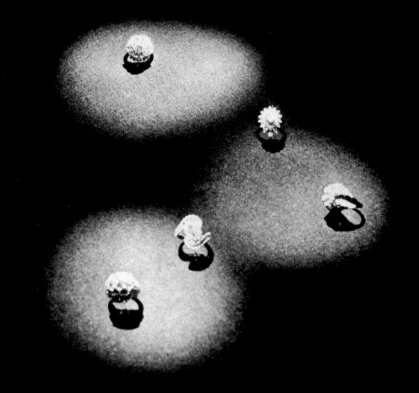

"When you don't grow up near the sea, that's when you start making magic about the sea. I first saw the sea when I came to New York City, and I return to it again and again.

"Seashells, like flowers, have no equal in design and color and mystery. To get the 'window' effect (looking from dark into light again), I used a black felt panel with a cutout framing the shell behind. One kind of lighting on the conch behind the black felt and another kind on the rings, which were mounted on the front of the black felt."

"Real fishhooks—a natural with real coral. But aligning the hooks and getting them to stay in line was no simple matter; it took a long time. One thing you have to be born with to be a window trimmer is patience."

"It takes imagination to see the graphic possibilities of old gloves! Robert Heitmann came to see me and showed me a whole bunch of old gloves he had been collecting. He said, 'I could make some marvelous things out of these.' He already visualized the fingers of the gloves as the cow's udders and wondered if there would be any objection. I reassured him, and so he went ahead, gluing down the gloves against felt backgrounds, with fabulous results. He handled the gloves so wonderfully—for instance, the way he turned the fingers up to make the feathers on the crane beside the cow."

145

EASTER

"To make the hat, I started with a chicken-wire frame. I nailed it onto the head and then I started placing eggs on top of it and gluing them together. When I finally got it all done, and all the eggs were really set—I hoped—I took the hat off the frame, thinking it was going to go pfft! But it didn't; it all held together, which was amazing. And on it there's a bird's nest, with real eggs in it. That hat had to have something that gave it oomph, and what could do it except a bird's nest? There was a very large diamond flower in there somewhere. You can see it better in the Life *photograph, where a live model is wearing the hat. The basket is made out of eggs, glued together, because a basket is what everybody puts eggs into."*

Life, April 12, 1963.
Photograph illustrating
article "Tiffany Topper
Tops Them All"

"All those eggs were suspended on nylon thread. There is a nylon thread that is so fine that you can hardly see it to tie a knot. That was a job! It looks simple, but just hanging the eggs, one by one, on three poles and trying to get a balance took two weeks of work. I did it upstairs in the workshop. Then while we were carrying the three poles downstairs, the threads got all tangled up and we had to stop and untangle them. And untangling them again when we finally put them in the window took hours.

"A tiny fan kept the eggs in continual motion. I like inanimate things that move—to give life to things that have no life of their own."

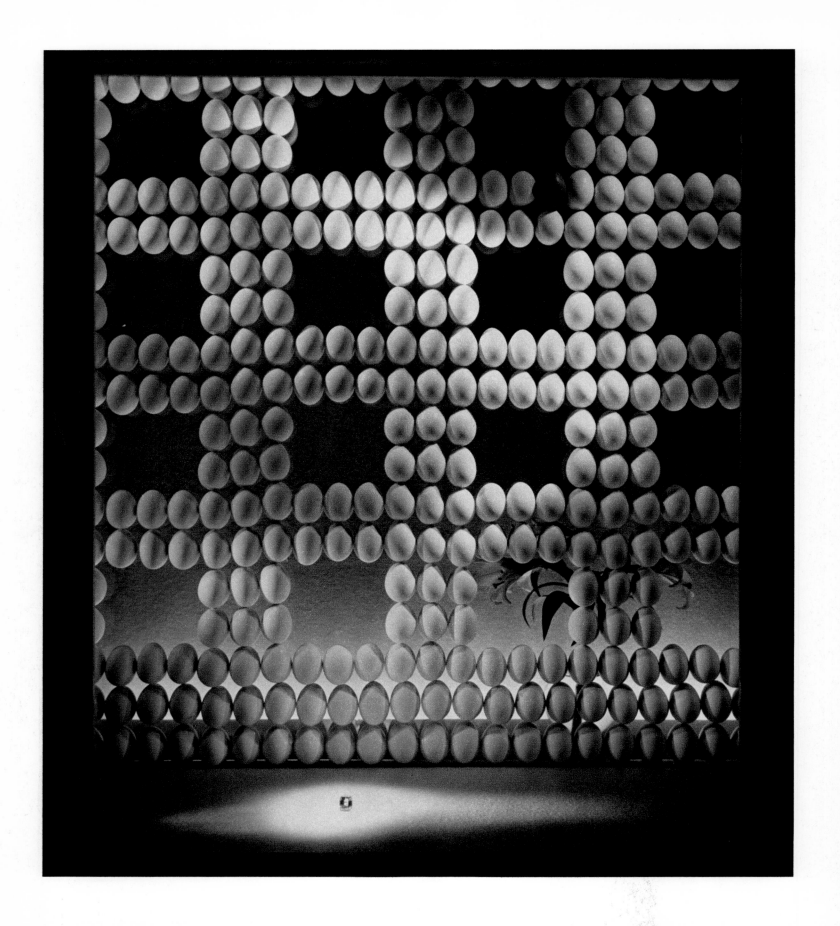

"This was the Easter I got very geometric. The eggs were glued onto plate glass. It was the only way I could possibly do them; otherwise they would never have held. Just very simple geometric patterns, as geometric as you can get, set off by the unevenness of the eggs. Because no two eggs have exactly the same shape. That imperfection is what pleases the eye."

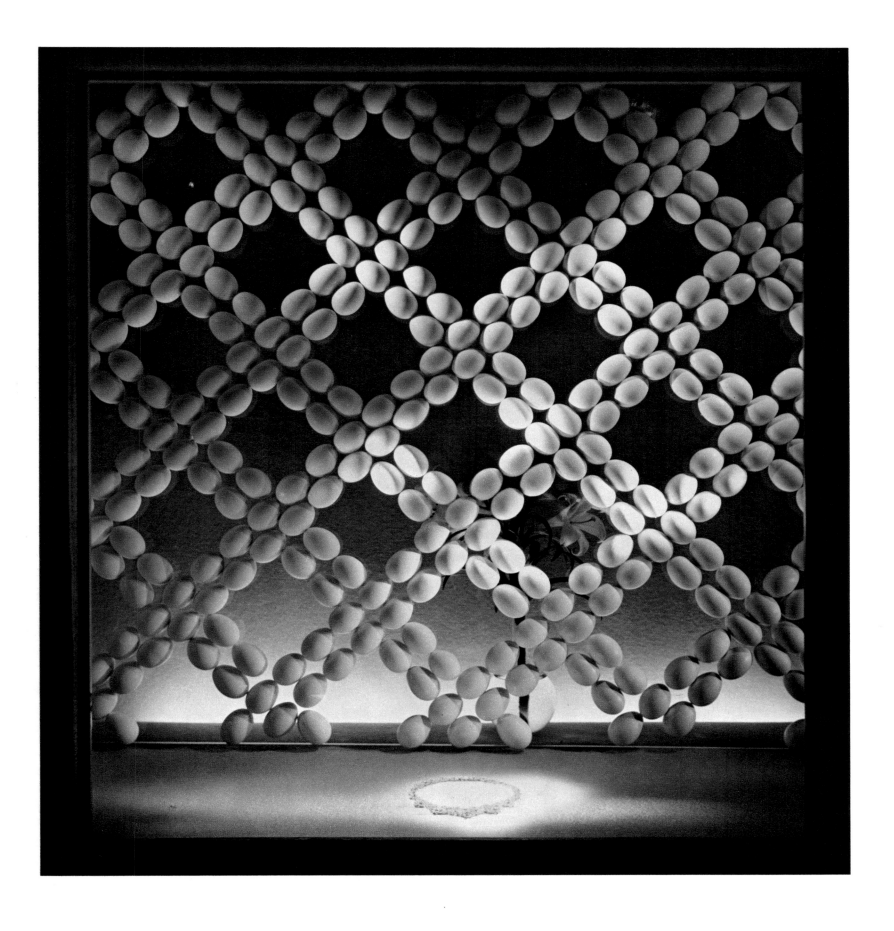

"The first of every year at least ten phone calls come from people who want to show me their painted eggs for Easter windows. I'm so tired of saying I don't like painted eggs; they're fine in Russia and Czechoslovakia and all those places, but not for me. I admire the craftsmanship of Fabergé eggs, but I don't particularly like the designs. Little gifty things for the Empress. I like eggs just the way they come out of the hen. There is something so pure about eggs."

"Almost every Easter I put real grass in the front two windows. There is just something about seeing real live grass at that time of year. I start in January—I go to a florist and say, 'Grow me some grass, please.' I keep it wet and it grows like crazy. We have to get in and chop it down with a scissors when it grows too tall."

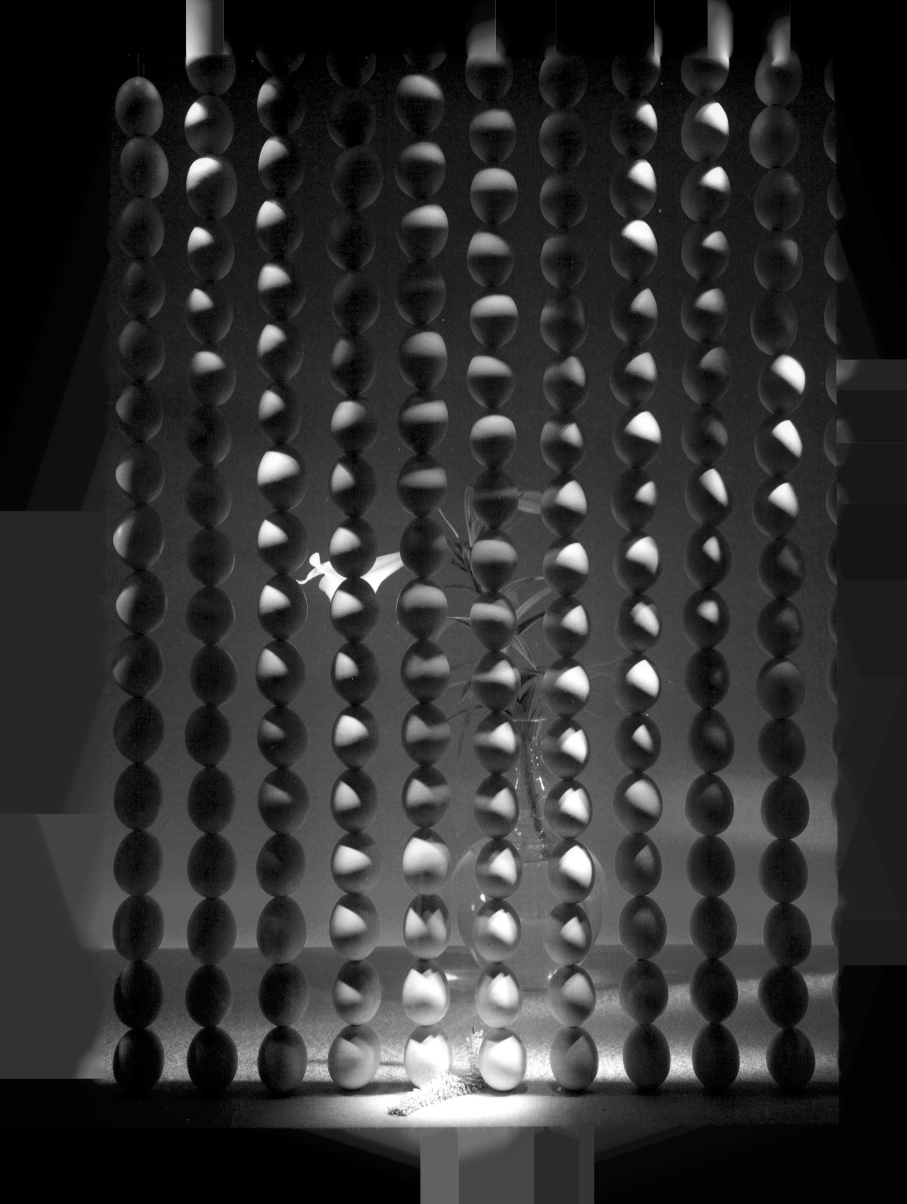

"It's the juxtaposition of light and dark again. Looking through something to see something else: you have to look through the curtain of eggs, which were glued up against the glass, to see the Easter lily."

"It was a pretty window, but one of those that make you very nervous because you're never quite sure they will work. There were more than five hundred blown-out eggs in it. Every one of those eggs was glued to chicken wire. That took weeks to do. And it was really concave, curving from nothing at the bottom to twenty-two inches deep at the top. I thought it would take a miracle to get it into the window. We put the butterflies and merchandise in first. Then we slowly slid the whole thing into the window and prayed—a lot!"

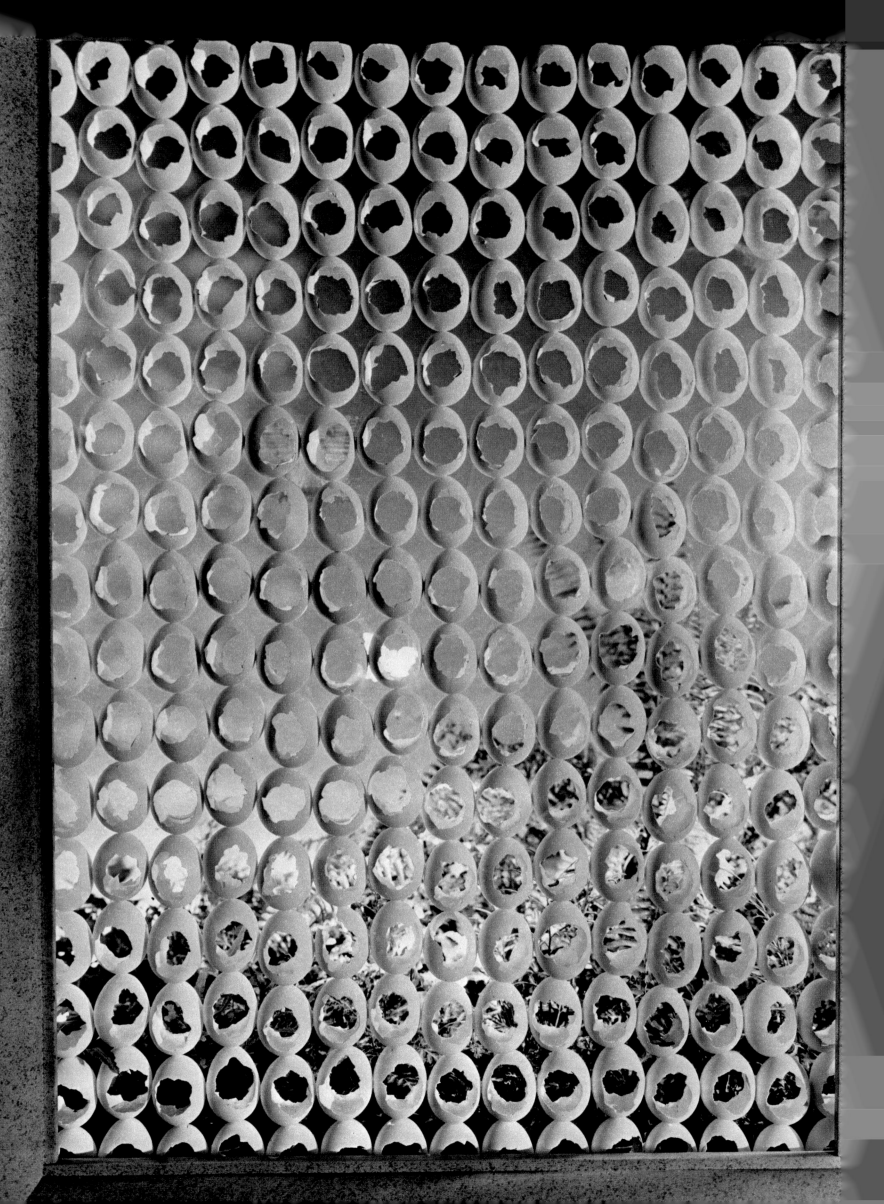

"You never know how an egg is going to break, and the variety of the contours of the break is much more beautiful than a photograph can show. The broken whole eggs were glued together, and through them delicate ferns and clover could be seen. One egg was left unbroken—to please the eye and catch the attention."

"A rhinoceros walking on eggs! And with egg on his horn, if not on his face...."

"These were the 'Cook yourself an omelette, honey, or fry yourself an egg, so long as you get a diamond out of it' windows."

"Half eggshells, with their edges all different, since they never break the same way, make a beautiful design when you put them together. These were all glued to a piece of felt. We laid the felt down flat, and we glued the eggs onto it, all the time thinking, 'When we pick it up, what's going to happen?' Nothing did."

FORM
AND
FANTASY

"Wheat is so beautiful! Getting the individual stalks of wheat to stand up is an old display trick. For each one, I drove a long pin into the floor, cut off its head, and stuck the stalk onto it. The idea of cutting down some of the wheat only occurred to me when I was actually working in the window. I had to have something to put the merchandise on, and that was the only thing I could do, given the shallow depth. Knowing I was going to use wheat, I had borrowed the sickle.

"The sheaves of wheat were no problem. I just tied a string around each sheaf and spread the base so that it could stand all by itself."

"The bamboo family has many varieties and they all have something about them that is mysterious and exotic. And no matter what you do with them, they look wonderful. You can arrange them in so many different ways."

"Bamboo is a beautifully designed thing. It's the irregularity that makes it so attractive; the space between two joints is never the same. Every interval is different from every other."

"The large piece of bamboo is about four and a half inches in diameter, I would say. I didn't even know bamboo grew that large. It gave me a chance to play with circles. I like circles, but geometry can get dull. I wish more painters would realize that. Something was needed to stop the eye, and that's what the bracelet does."

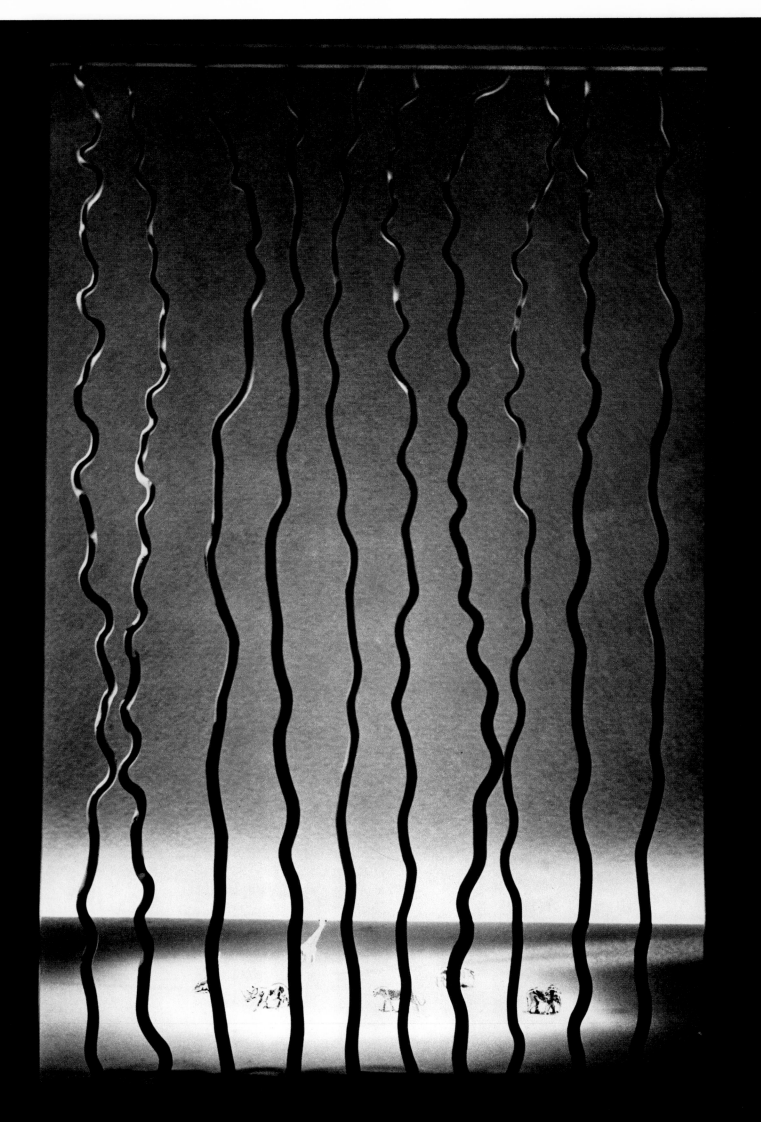

"*These curly sticks—very strange, very white, and very beautiful—come from Japan. They're called* unyru, *and the florist says they're made from the wisteria vine. With all the gold-and-stone animals behind them, they really look like the bars of a cage in some crazy zoo.*"

"*I was barren of ideas, and I knew I had to do a set of windows in two days. So I said to my assistant, 'Let's go downtown to Little Italy and walk around and see what happens.' We passed a shop that had nothing but pasta in the windows; it looked absolutely beautiful. And I said, 'Now I know what we're going to do. Let's buy some pasta.' So I bought five pounds of practically everything, and the Italian lady looked at me like 'You're crazy!' She said, 'What you gonta do with all this?' I said, 'A window display.' She said, 'Where?' I said, 'At Tiffany's.' She said, 'Where's that?' I said, 'Fifty-seventh Street and Fifth Avenue. Haven't you ever seen it?' 'No,' she said, 'I never heard of it.'*

"*The pasta windows made the cover of the pasta trade magazine. Imagine, an article on Tiffany windows in* Macaroni Journal!"

"In the airport, returning from London in 1963, I saw a kid eating an ice-cream cone and thought, 'Mmm. Isn't that nice? I'll do ice-cream cones.' The next morning I said to my assistant, 'Get ahold of somebody at Nabisco and have them give me a couple of thousand ice-cream cones because I want to do some windows.' Well, they sent me the cones and I started playing with them, breaking quite a few because they're very fragile. Mostly, we glued them together in sections and suspended the ones that couldn't stand up by themselves. Some of the effects reminded me of Gaudí's fantastic architecture. And turned upside down, the cones made marvelous holders for rings and bracelets!"

"*First came the fabrics, then the stuffed animals. They were made by Edith La Bate, a talented Brazilian who was just the one to make some creatures with character to them. The frog was my favorite—he was green and white, and the fabric so suited being made into a frog. It didn't occur to me until afterward that I might have been influenced by the French artist Édouard Vuillard, who often painted patterns against patterns.*"

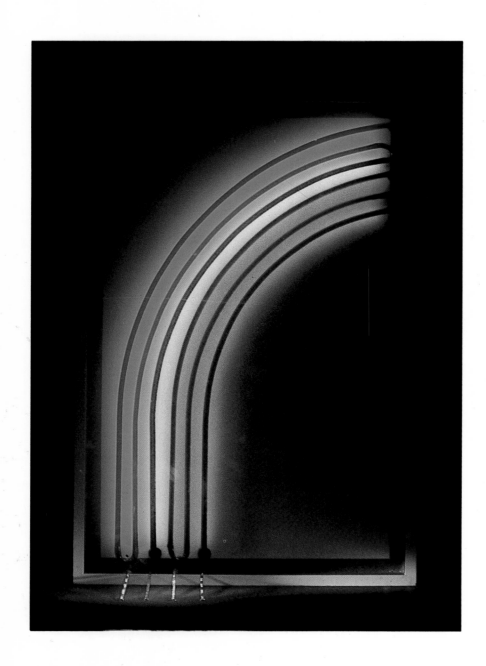

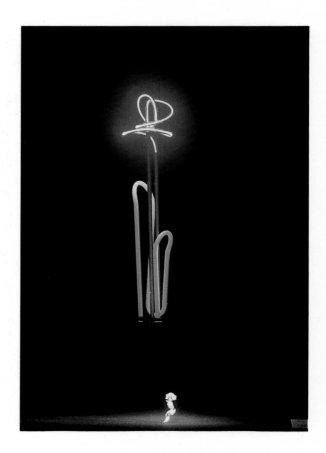

"*This is the only time I've ever used neon in my windows. I loved the rainbow thing with all the different colors. And the paint pouring out of that can, with the rubies and diamonds! Both the artist—Yukio John Tanaka—and Tiffany's received awards (on the local, regional, and national levels) from the Lighting Design Awards Program of the Illuminating Engineering Society. I understand this is the only time the awards have been given for window display.*"

"A company sent me a sample of a new sponge-rubber material that is used under carpeting. When I started working with it I discovered that if I filled the jars with water it would magnify the pattern and change the whole look of the thing. Without the magnification, it would have been pretty dull. We found that we couldn't use city water because you get a residue around the edge. So we used bottled spring water, and we had to replenish it daily. Every morning, seven-thirty, fill the jars. Water the water!"

"The keys are very old. I found a whole box of them in a junk shop out in the country. They're all rusty, a beautiful color. I just glued them down on a piece of plate glass. I use plate glass a lot for things like this. It's much better than trying to suspend something. With suspension you can never keep things straight. All the keys are different, and they're all going in the same direction, except one. That's an old trick of mine to see if people are looking."

"They make spools out of plastic now—not only plastic but gold plastic. I called a man at Coats & Clark and said, 'I love your spools, especially the wooden ones. I would like to do something with them in the windows.' He was thrilled and sent me hundreds and hundreds of spools of both kinds, with and without thread on them. I had a wonderful time with them. The ones with colored and black-and-white thread were very effective with jewels picking up the same tones."

"The wooden spools made a marvelous patterned background when fitted together, row on row. All those spools were held together with glue. So were the spools that made up the Leaning Tower of Pisa, which really did lean, and the spools doing the impossible balancing act."

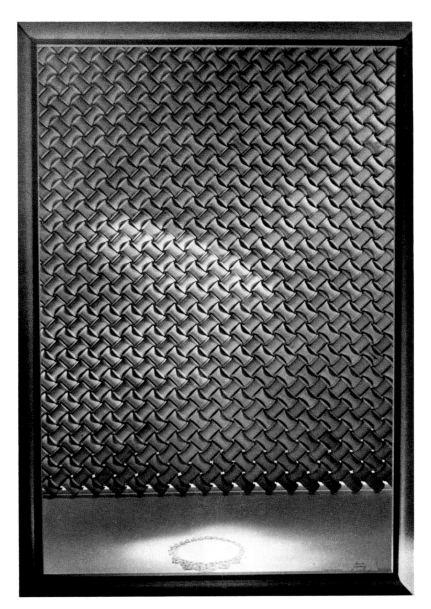

"The staple gun is the greatest tool that any displayman has. Without it, I don't know how he'd get along. When I started in display there were no staple guns. To cover panels, you had to work with a bunch of tacks in your mouth and a magnetic hammer. You learned to spit the tacks out, raise the hammer, and boom! You could really work fast that way, once you learned the trick, but not as fast as with the staple gun."

"This was from a set of, shall we call them, handiwork windows. There was a knitting one and a crochet one and an embroidery one, and this was the crochet one. The hands are holding the crochet needle, and I had a friend of mine who crochets do exactly the same design in crochet thread as the necklace had. So crochet yourself a necklace!"

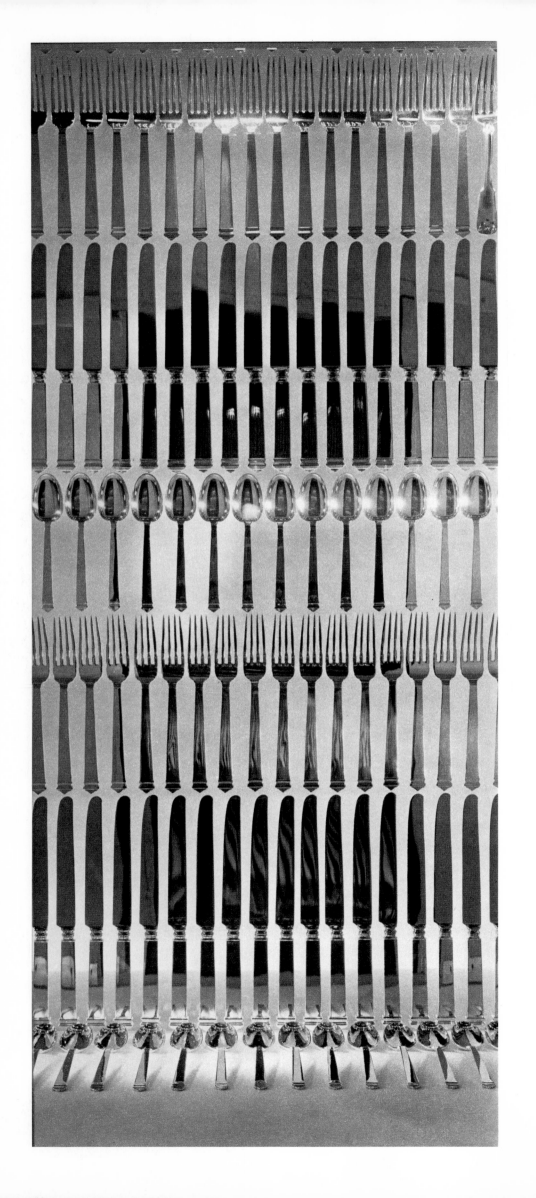

"The plate glass technique again. I wanted to do a window on flatware, and the only way I could get it all standing up straight was to glue the flatware onto a piece of plate glass. So, I glued a row of forks, a row of knives, a row of spoons, a row of forks, a row of knives, a row of spoons, and I cut the window's width down, to make less gluing. There's a wrong fork there; it's not the same pattern. The old trick again, to see if observers are really observing."

"Another long, narrow window —to cut down on gluing! The goblets aren't against plate glass but I did have to glue them together so they would stand up. There was a certain suspense, wondering if they would fall."

"There was no more graphic way of showing Elsa Peretti's Diamonds-By-The-Yard, I figured, than making a lattice of yardsticks and then just suspending her diamonded chains on it. What are diamonds by the yard except a yard of diamonds, and what do you use to measure a yard with except a yardstick?"

"The famous little pendent bottle by Elsa Peretti, in which a real flower could be worn because it held water, inspired this window. Arranging the bottles was a week-long chore—tying them with that fine nylon thread, stapling the thread to a rod, and finally transporting the whole thing gingerly from the workshop down to the window. Then when it was all set up in the window, it was pretty—the composition was all right—but it didn't have any life to it. So each morning on my way to work I stopped by a florist's and picked up a rose. That one live flower made a great difference."

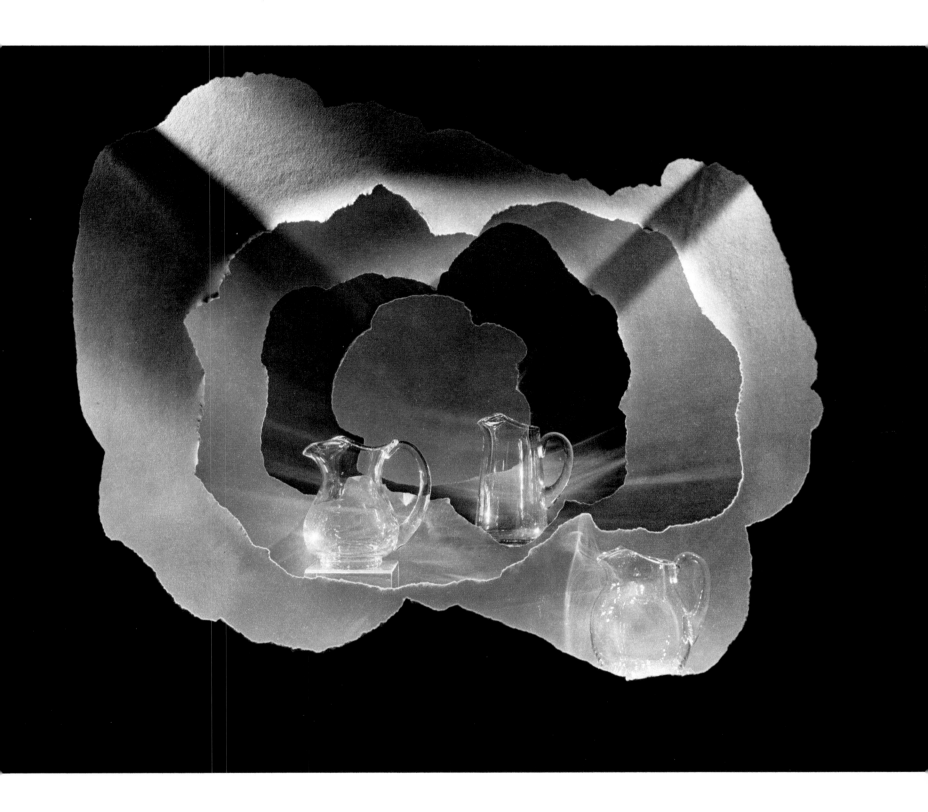

"The spiderweb was made of gold thread on a frame in the workshop. Unfastening the web from the frame and fastening it in the window took some doing! I couldn't have a frame showing; I wanted it to look as if the spider had woven its web right there."

"This was a matter of mounting paper on frames—four frames, four layers of paper. I stretched the paper on the frames upstairs in the workshop and put them in the window one at a time. Put in the first one, tear it. Put in the second one, tear it to go with the first one, and so on. Afterward I was amazed, because I could only see what I was doing in the reflection in the glass."

"In these windows I was trying to cut designs to follow the pattern of the jewelry I was using; this time the merchandise was the jumping-off point. I loved doing this; I cut all these out with my own two hands. The interesting thing about the paper chain is that I cut all the links out with pinking shears, so that each one has a decorative shape. It's fantastic what you can do with paper."

"People like looking through windows, particularly someone else's. I wanted these to make viewers feel they were looking through windows and seeing the scene—in Spoleto and in Venice (the onion domes on top of San Marco). So I used black shutters as frames for the black-and-white photographs. I had taken them on a trip to Italy. There's also a view looking up into the dome of the Galleria in Milan. They're blown up very large, six by five feet."

CHRISTMAS

"Creating a fantasy is one of the joys of life. I wanted to do an orchestra of gold and enameled animals playing their instruments in the woods. I said to Bob Rauschenberg and Jasper Johns, 'Look, I want to do a forest. I want bare trees, but I want them to look like they have ice on them.' They used the same trick that I do with Duco; it dries and it looks like ice. They did it beautifully. Then I painted a backdrop of sky."

"The inspiration for the rococo window was a place I've never seen, the Amalienburg—a pleasure building on the grounds of the Nymphenburg Palace, near Munich. I had a book on it, in German, which I couldn't read, but the color photographs showed this marvelous pale sort of turquoisey-blue and silver ballroom, where everything was silver-leafed. I'd always wanted to see it, so I created my own Amalienburg. I had a whole set of miniature furniture, and I painted it. We made the wall decoration by squeezing plaster out of a pastry bag, and we silver-leafed it. Then I filled the room with Venetian furniture, crystal chandeliers, and mirrors. My assistant at the time was a wiz with the pastry bag."

"*Just as in a trompe l'oeil painting by Harnett, here everything becomes part of the whole picture—the unfinished needlepoint that I had a friend do for me, my favorite dolly (the one that looks like a Renoir), the sleigh bells, the wishbone (I have a box full of wishbones—turkey wishbones, chicken wishbones, the whole bit). I took a lot of the junk that I've saved downstairs on a tray and improvised in the window as I went along. The background was wood, like most of Harnett's, and I deepened the shadows of the objects with paint. Even the merchandise became part of the picture.*"

"Like the windows themselves, which are meant to be viewed from right to left, starting on Fifth Avenue, these scenes go from right to left instead of left to right. In the beginning are the Three Wise Men, following the star. The second scene shows the people watching a puppet show featuring the Madonna and Child. A festive procession starts on the Fifty-seventh Street side. The people are all dressed up—they have a seventeenth-century look—and they are really celebrating the holiday."

"Stringing the popcorn for the curtain behind the vase took a month of three people's time. It was in four layers and five and a half to six feet high. The huge vase was eighteen and a half inches tall and held fourteen gallons of water. Full, we couldn't have lifted into the window; we had to siphon the water in and out. What that vase did was absolutely beautiful! Seen through the water, the popcorn took on another life, a life of its own—it was magnified and distorted. And the slight stirring of the air by a small fan added to the effect.

"The irregularity of popcorn shapes is very appealing. But you can't just put glue on pieces of popcorn and throw them around. You have to take each piece and glue, stick, glue, stick. Each piece had to be individually glued onto the popcorn snowman and onto the felt background behind the hibachi corn popper."

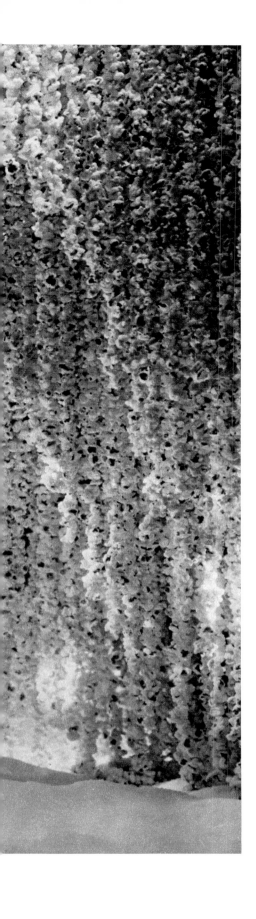

"Santa Claus is in his office, and all's right with the world. Two of his helpers are bringing in the mail, the shelves are well-stocked with toys, the head of the workshop stands ready to fill requests, and one of the reindeer has stuck his head through the door to supervise."

"On Christmas Day, Mr. and Mrs. Claus are seen enjoying some well-earned leisure, having tea and opening their presents in front of the fireplace. The mantel is decked with Christmas greens, and on either side hangs the portrait of a favorite reindeer. These glimpses of Santa's world were created by Robert Heitmann."

"Santa's fishing. Santa is made of papier-mâché. The ice took forever
to do because it was layer on layer on layer on layer of paraffin, which I
heated and poured. I put a little blue dye in it. And underneath there was
real water, which was moving (I always use a circulating pump).

"Santa was having good luck: that's a gold-and-diamond-and-peridot
fish he's caught."

"That wonderful reindeer really takes me back. He starred in the very
first set of Christmas windows that I did at Tiffany's."

"Every Christmas, the last window going east on Fifty-seventh Street celebrates New Year's and/or champagne. One year I made up, for that window, the story of a lady who had been skiing and had fallen into deep snow; she needs help and thrusts her hand up with a glass and there's a Saint Bernard waiting, not with a keg of brandy but with a bottle of champagne!

"That Saint Bernard was heaven. I got him from a display house, no longer existent, that did exceptional papier-mâché work. I said, 'I want a Saint Bernard, and I only want him from here up.' They were such perfectionists that where they cut him off, they painted all his insides. Back there, where you couldn't see it, was a cross section of a Saint Bernard."

LIST OF INSTALLATION DATES AND CREDITS

ACKNOWLEDGMENTS

At Tiffany & Co., over the years, I have been most fortunate in my associations. I am grateful to Mr. Walter Hoving for his understanding of my work and the freedom it requires; to Mr. Henry Platt for his encouragement and appreciation; and to Mr. Farnham Lefferts, President of the company during the seven years when I was Director of Design Development for Gold Jewelry, for making those years a pleasure. In that post I had the able assistance of designers Sonia Younis Hamra and Don Berg, who led me into research in new fields and who did much inspired work; of Veronica Stanion, who managed the department; of buyers Charles Dishman and Robert Swanson; and of the gifted gemologist William Tants, who taught me all I know about stones. Currently, designers Angela Cummings and Elsa Peretti are a constant inspiration to me, not only through their work but through the exchange of ideas in our wide-ranging conversations.

In New York I have been blessed with the help and friendship of many in the arts, design, theater, dance, and photography, as well as in display. Among fellow displaymen, I owe special thanks to Jim Buckley, Gene McCabe, and Robert Currie. From Joe Schwartz I learned about jewelry manufacture and its limits; from Pablo Manzoni, the makeup expert, how to make up my mannequins. Cris Alexander taught me all about photography, and Richard Avedon (who lent me his studio at one time) and Milton H. Greene have been generous and influential mentors. The dancer David Nillo of Ballet Theater sparked my interest in ballet, an interest enlarged by my work with dancer–choreographers John Butler and Paul Taylor. My lighting has been strongly influenced by the luminous paintings of Loren MacIver and by the genius of the late Jean Rosenthal, probably the greatest of all lighting experts. It has been my privilege to work with many exceptional artists, among them Gyo Fujikawa, Barbara Gould, Patrick Sullivan, Roger Sammis, Robert Heitmann, E.J. Taylor, Jeanne Owens, and George and June Grammer. I treasure my experience, in May 1970, of designing and installing the permanent exhibition "Gold of the Americas" at the American Museum of Natural History, which brought me into contact with the eminent and delightful Dr. Junius Bird, Curator of South American Archaeology, and with Sue (Mrs. John) Tishman, who worked so effectively with us for the success of the project. Earlier, in 1964, I had had the pleasure of working with John and Nora Wise, installing their collection of Pre-Columbian gold in the "World of Ancient Gold" exhibit at the World's Fair.

Many professionals in the trade have furthered my career through their understanding and encouragement, most especially the designers Pauline Trigère and George Stavropoulos; Martin Feinstein, formerly head of promotion for Hurok Attractions; editor Babs Simpson, formerly at *Vogue* and now at *House & Garden*; publicist Virginia Haynes, formerly at Kenneth's; and Fred and Ethel Rathe, display manufacturers.

Abroad, I have had the cooperation and gained the friendship of many outstanding jewelry manufacturers and designers: Mr. and Mrs. Henri Stern of Patek Philippe Watches in Geneva; Mr. and Mrs. Karl Scheufele of Chopard Watches in Geneva; Mr. and Mrs. Jean-Pierre Ecoffey, Geneva; Mr. and Mrs. Marcello Falai, Lucetta Rapi, and Luana Cinti in Florence; Hanns Krahmer in Frankfort; and Mr. and Mrs. Georges Lenfant in Paris. In Paris, Simone Racine of the American Export Company has been wonderfully helpful. In London, during the production of *The Ides of March*, I was lucky in being able to call on the talents of Noel Howard, who supervised the costume making, and of Sam Kirkpatrick, who executed the props and has since made many marvelous constructions for my windows. And it was a delight to work with Sir John Gielgud and Irene Worth, who have remained good friends.

No list of those to whom I feel indebted would be complete without the names of my close friends Mr. and Mrs. Allan Wild, William Rondina, Dr. Alex Sahagian-

Edwards, Gino DiGrandi, and Hughes De Montalembert.

Something that is most important to the success of any display director is having a truly good assistant, and I have been exceptionally lucky in this respect, starting with Walter Hazeltine during my first few years at Bonwit Teller's. Walter was a brilliant, creative person with a love for humanity and an irrepressible sense of fun. We worked together like a pair of crazy twins, playing out our comedies, romantic fantasies, and social commentaries in our windows, often switching roles as "straight man."

Later Dan Arje was my assistant at Bonwit's—good, gentle, sharp as a tack, and ever reliable. We worked together for the remainder of my years there, and he took over as display director when I left, at the end of 1961.

During my twenty-five years at Tiffany's I've had three assistants, all named Ronald. When I first came, I fell heir to Ron Prybycien, who was young (twenty-one) and eager and had a marvelous facility with his hands. I enjoyed teaching a young person, and we did some great things together. When he had to leave to do his stint in the Army in 1951, I persuaded Ron McNamer to come to Tiffany's from Bonwit's, and we worked together for the two years that Prybycien was in the service. McNamer was immensely creative and could turn his hand to anything; he seemed a natural for jewelry design, and I made this suggestion to Mr. Hoving. So he was sent to Italy to study and subsequently was very successful in designing jewelry for Tiffany's. He is now a designer for the well-known jeweler Zolotas in Athens. When, in 1961, Ron Prybycien embarked upon his own enterprise, "Accents and Images," in New York, I asked Ron Smith, who had been my secretary at Bonwit's, if he would like to be my assistant at Tiffany's. We've worked together now for nineteen years. Ron can build anything and has learned all I know about lighting. We are a very organized team, working almost as one mind with two pairs of hands.

For this book I must thank Judith Goldman, whose text is a discerning synthesis of hours of interviews. At Harry N. Abrams, Inc., I am beholden to Lena Tabori for shepherding this project, and to Ruth Eisenstein for editing it with care and taste. I especially appreciate the enthusiasm and stamina of Dirk Luykx, who conceived the project, gathered up an excellent representation from a wealth of material, taped my commentaries, and managed to put it all into a splendid design.

Gene Moore
June 1980

BIBLIOGRAPHY

BOOKS AND CATALOGUES

Emory, Michael. *Windows.* Chicago: Contemporary Books, Inc., 1977, pp. [14, 16, 30], figs. 32, 33, 35–39, 56–59, 65–67, 83–85, 94–96, 105–107, 139, 140.

Gaba, Lester. *The Art of Window Display.* New York and London: Studio Publications with T. Y. Crowell Co., 1952, pp. 29, 55, 65, 74.

Gold of the Americas: An Exhibit of Pre-Columbian Gold..., New York: American Museum of Natural History, p. [2].

Goldwater, Robert, in collaboration with René d'Harnoncourt. *Modern Art in Your Life* (Museum of Modern Art Bulletin, vol. xvii, no. 1, 1949), p. 39.

Herdeg, Walter H. (ed.). *Window Display (Schaufensterkunst; L'art de l'étalage),* vol. 2. Zurich: Graphis Press, 1961, figs. 219–228.

Knapp, Walter (ed.). *Schaufenster International 2: Window Display,* New York: Hastings House, 1973, figs. 1, 7, 10, 13, 52, 57, 64–70, 73, 74.

Marcus, Leonard S. *The American Store Window.* New York: Whitney Library of Design (an imprint of Watson Guptill Publications); London: The Architectural Press Ltd., pp. 44, 45, 50, 54, 74–77, 76, 119–125, 144–153.

Purcell, Joseph. *The Tiffany Touch,* New York: Random House, 1971, pp. 192, 271–276.

Schaufenster: (exhib. cat.), Stuttgart: Württembergischer Kunstverein Stuttgart, 1974, p. 56, 4 ills.

Sculpture in Time and Place (exhib. cat.). New York: Sculptors Guild, Inc., 1952, p. 12

Sieber, Roy. *African Textiles and Decorative Arts* (exhib. cat.). New York: Museum of Modern Art, 1972 (exhibition installed by Gene Moore).

Thomajan, P.K. (ed.). *Gene Moore/Bonwit Teller (Design and Paper 28).* New York: Marquardt & Company, [c. 1948], 14 pp., 17 ills. incl. cover.

Tomkins, Calvin. *Off the Wall: Robert Rauschenberg and the Art World of Our Time,* New York: Doubleday & Co., 1980, pp. 54, 66, 111, 113, 114, 131–132, 140, 176–178.

ARTICLES (listed chronologically)

" 'Robbery' in Windows Holds Up Traffic," *Women's Wear Daily,* July 23, 1946.

"Don Freeman's Newsstand Watches a Fifth Avenue Window Dresser at Work," *PM,* December 9, 1948.

"Behind the Glass," *Time,* December 27, 1948. p. 37.

"Gene Moore—en mesterdekoratør på 5th Avenue," *Dansk Reklame* (Copenhagen), April 4, 1949, p. 52.

Moore, Gene. "A Star Is Born at Bonwit's," *Display World,* July 1951, pp. 18–19, 63, 9 ills. incl. cover.

"Uses Dramatic Simplicity in Window Displays," *Women's Wear Daily,* March 2, 1955.

Robertson, Nan. "Hare-brained Rabbits in Bonwit's Are the Result of Serious Thought," *New York Times,* March 23, 1956.

Robertson, Nan. "Tiny Store Windows Show Jewels in Fantasy Settings," *New York Times,* November 21, 1956.

"Diamond Yolk," *Newsweek,* August 26, 1957, p. 78.

Pauley, Gay. "Former Chicago Fine Arts Student Dreams Up Wild, Crowd-stopping Displays." *Gary* [Indiana] *Post-Tribune,* December 27, 1957.

"The Way to Display as Seen by the Experts: Gene Moore," *Home Furnishings Daily,* April 7, 1958, Sec. 2, p. 16.

Berger, Meyer. "About New York: Window Artist Delves into the Unorthodox in Glittering Displays at Tiffany's," *New York Times,* May 2, 1958.

"Old Rocks in a New Role," *Sports Illustrated,* August 11, 1958, pp. E 3–4, 5 ills.

Kayser, Alf. "Tiffany Displays Wish-Dreams," *Graphis* (Zurich), January/February 1960, pp. 22–27, 5 ills.

"Aussergewohnliche Dekorationen," *Gold + Silber, Uhren + Schmuck,* April 1960, pp. 34–35, 5 ills.

"Studio's Gastenboek: Gene Moore, Tiffany, New York," *Studio* (Rotterdam), September 7, 1960, pp. 196–198, 3 ills incl. cover.

Lee, Tom. "Gene Moore," *Graphis* (Zurich), November/December 1960, pp. 528–333, 14 ills.

Wilcox, Lee. "Meet Gene Moore," *House Beautiful,* December 1960, pp. 126–127, 170–172, 1 ill.

Wheeler, Geoffrey. "The Fine Art of Winning Windows," *National Jeweler,* May 1962, pp. 69–72.

"Gene Moore's Art Screens," *New York Herald Tribune,* May 23, 1962.

Hahn, Vera. "Tiffany's Moore Etches Image of Store by Windows' Contrast," *Home Furnishings Daily,* August 17, 1962.

"Macaroni at Tiffany's," *The Macaroni Journal,* October 1962.

"Fiber Marketing Exhibit Wins Decorating Award," *Allied Chemical News,* December 7, 1962, p. 1, 1 ill.

Eisenberg, Howard and Arlene. "The World's Largest Audience," *Cosmopolitan,* December 1962, pp. 72–78.

"A Tiffany Topper Tops Them All," *Life,* April 12, 1963, pp. A 10–11, 1 ill.

"Diamonds Are a 'Cone's Best Friend,'" *Nabisco Magazine,* October 1963, pp. 8–9, 9 ills. incl. cover.

Warren, Virginia Lee. "Display Director's Windows Are Works of Art," *New York Times,* February 27, 1965.

Franklin, Rebecca. "Alabama's Gene Moore Brightens Easter Parade," *New York Daily News,* April 18, 1965.

"Engaging the Eye," *Jewelers Circular—Keystone* (Philadelphia), April 1965, pp. 106, 108, 2 ills.

Saarinen, Aline. "Windows on Fifth Avenue," *Show,* April 1965, pp. 16–21, 7 ills.

Cunningham, Bill. "The Most Ravishing Show in New York Is FREE...," *Chicago Tribune,* July 19, 1965.

Metzner, Remolo. "Air Flows Like Water," *New York Journal–American,* August 5, 1965.

Caputo, Livio. "Tiffany Innaffia i brillianti col gin," *Epoca* (Milan), August–September 1965, pp. 78–81.

van Maasdijk, H. R. "Gene Moore, de illusionist van Fifth Avenue," *Ariadne* (Amsterdam), September 29, 1965, pp. 980–982, 9 ills.

"No! No! No! This Is Not Precious City Water," *The Seagram Spotlight,* November 1965, pp. 18–21.

Spaak, Eleanor. "Gene Moore—Display Genius," *Home Furnishings Daily,* December 3, 1965.

Spaak, Eleanor. "Gene Moore—His World, His Work," *Home Furnishings Daily,* December 10, 1965.

"Vitrinen bei Tiffany," *Die Schaulade* (Bamberg, West Germany), February 1966, pp. 270–271, 4 ills.

"The Year New York Dried Up," *The Sunday Times Magazine* (London), February 13, 1966, pp. 16–17, 1 ill.

"The Windows at Tiffany's," *National Jeweler,* October 1966, pp. 71–73, 8 ills.

"Meet Gene Moore," *Home Furnishings Daily,* October 7, 1966, pp. 6, 8, 12.

"The World's Greatest Window Trimmer—Gene Moore," *Display World,* December 1966, pp. 35–37, 77, 79, 81, 9 ills. incl. cover.

"Who Else Would Think of a Safety Pin with Diamonds?," *New York Times,* May 11, 1967.

Spaak, Eleanor. "Gene Moore...His Moment," *Home Furnishings Daily,* June 9, 1967.

Bengtson, Carolyn. "Tiffany's: Those Sparkling Show Windows Works of Art," *Austin* [Texas] *Statesman,* July 21, 1967.

Sheppard, Eugenia. "The IN Safety Pin," *San Francisco Chronicle,* August 2, 1967.

Hart-Green, Cherie. "The Tiffany Man," *Women's Wear Daily,* July 3, 1968.

Cunningham, Bill. "When Tiffany & Co. in Manhattan Holds Its Own Kind of a Flower Show You Can Expect Something Special," *Chicago Tribune,* July 15, 1968.

"Créé pour Tiffany," *L'Oeil* (Lausanne), November 1968, pp. 40–47.

"The Light of Christmas," *House & Garden,* December 1968, p. 53, 1 ill.

"Make 'Em Look," *Women's Wear Daily,* June 3, 1969, p. 42.

Cunningham, Bill. "For Easter Windows, Lots of Eggshells Are Crackling at Tiffany & Co. in New York City," *Chicago Tribune,* March 23, 1970.

"Kenneth's Winning Windows," *Cosmetics Fair,* June 1971, pp. 26–27, 9 ills.

"International Shop Report: USA," *Inspiration 41* (Zurich), June 15, 1971, figs. 51, 52.

"Around the World in Display: USA," *Inspiration 42* (Zurich), August 15, 1971, figs. 91–94.

"U.S. Display Report," *Inspiration 49* (Zurich), October 16, 1972, figs. 28–32.

"Gene Moore: The Legendary Window Trimmer," *Corset, Bra & Lingerie Magazine,* January 1974, p. 16.

Jones, Joyce. "He's Tiffany's Main Man," *Sunday Daily Record,* April 21, 1974.

Bond, Linda Thorsen. "Small Wonders," *Women's Wear Daily,* April 23, 1974.

"Creator of Tiffany Display Toasts Passing Parade," *New York Times,* December 11, 1975.

Stevens, Carol. "Tiffany Windows," *Print,* May/June 1976, pp. 48–53 and cover.

Gray, Margaret. "An Interview with Gene Moore," *Visual Merchandising,* July 1976, pp. 25–27, 7 illus.

Anderson, Dorrine. "The Tiffany-Hoving Touch," *No. 1: The Magazine of Hertz,* July 1976, pp. 3–5, 1 ill.

"Inspiration Academy: New Members... Gene Moore," *Inspiration 75* (Zurich), February/March 1977, p. [7], 1 ill.

Pippos, Gerald. "Those Fabulous Fifties," *Visual Merchandising,* June 1977, p. 66.

Carlsen, Peter. "Design/Gene Moore & Bob Currie," *Avenue,* June–July 1979, pp. 68–72.

Jordan, Helen Bohn. "Tiffany's Tiny Window Rooms," *Christian Science Monitor,* August 21, 1979.

"All the Best Around the World: United States, Tiffany & Co., New York... Gene Moore, Display Director," *Inspiration 91* (Zurich), October/November 1979.

"Trend '80: Magic Visual Fascination," *Inspiration 93* (Zurich, Atlanta), February/March 1980, 5 ills.

INDEX

PHOTOGRAPH CREDITS

Numbers refer to pages on which the photographs are reproduced. All sources listed are located in New York.

Leland Cook: 9, 68–71, 207; Susan Cook: 44; Fifth Avenue Display Photographers: 73, 121, 128, 144–46, 151, 158, 177, 180, 181, 184; Bob Gomel, Life, © 1963 Time Inc.: 149 (bottom); Seth Joel: 8, 12, 125; Nick Malan Studio, Inc.: 20, 23, 29, 32, 36, 39, 50, 62, 63, 67, 77, 81, 82, 88–91, 93–95, 104, 105, 107–9, 112, 113, 119, 120, 132–36, 138, 139, 148, 149 (top), 152, 153, 155, 160, 162, 163, 165, 168, 170, 172, 174–76, 178, 179, 182, 183, 185–88, 190–93, 196, 197, 199, 202, 206, 208–11, 213–15; Jerry P. Melmed: 17, 45, 86, 98, 102, 103, 124, 159; Gene Moore: 52–55; Lee Prescott: 38, 87, 99; Retail Reporting Bureau: 37; Virginia Roehl Studio: 22, 27, 30, 31, 51–53, 56–58, 60, 61, 66, 74, 84, 85, 96, 97, 100, 106, 110, 111, 114–18, 122, 123, 126, 127, 129–31, 137, 140–43, 157, 161, 164, 166, 169, 171, 173, 189, 194–98, 200, 201, 204, 205, 212, 216; Tiffany & Co.: 40, 41.